Reawakening HOPE

THE MISSION OF A MOTHERLESS CHILD

Kingsley Chukwuemeka Ihejirika, PhD

WESTBOW
PRESS®
A DIVISION OF THOMAS NELSON
& ZONDERVAN

WestBow Press books may be ordered through booksellers or by contacting:

WestBow Press
A Division of Thomas Nelson & Zondervan
1663 Liberty Drive
Bloomington, IN 47403
www.westbowpress.com
844-714-3454

ISBN: 978-1-6642-4495-5 (sc)
ISBN: 978-1-6642-4497-9 (hc)
ISBN: 978-1-6642-4496-2 (e)

Library of Congress Control Number: 2021918904

Print information available on the last page.

WestBow Press rev. date: 10/26/2021

Contents

CHAPTER ONE

A Motherless Childhood

Thirteen months after I was born, my mother died. I grew up motherless with all the challenges associated with that. My earliest developmental recollections were from mid to late childhood. It was very hard to realize that, unlike most kids my age, I had no one that I could call *Mother*. I didn't know what my mother looked like until I was almost nine. At that time, my older brother Chieke, who was a student at the Katolieke Universiteit Leuven in Belgium, was visiting Nigeria on vacation. He had brought the only surviving photograph of my mother home with him. The rest had been destroyed during the Nigerian Civil War of 1967, a period in which most families, including mine, lost more than one million loved ones and valuable properties.

The very first day when I was privileged to have a glance at what my mother looked like turned out to be quite dramatic. Chieke had given that photograph of her, which he had guarded so carefully, to my aunt Violet. While she and a couple of other relatives were in our living room admiring it, I walked in. Immediately, they handed that photograph to me and asked if I could tell whose image it was. Unsurprisingly, I was unable to tell that the person in it was my mother. I had thought and guessed that the photograph was of my aunt, given that she looked very much like the person in the photograph. But I was quick to realize, due to the looks on their faces, that I had just seen my mother and failed to recognize her. I spent the remainder of that day in sorrow and grief. I have kept a copy of that photograph with me ever since.

Despite my amazing relationship with my father, my childhood was still quite challenging. Growing up without a mother was one of the worst experiences imaginable. I went from one foster home to another in search of a place where I could feel loved. Sometimes I felt accepted, and at other times, I felt lonely in a crowd. A lot of people who knew me then might feel quite surprised hearing this, since I mostly seemed cheerful. But that was only a façade. There was always a feeling of sickening loneliness inside me. I was not sure that I could be myself without being rejected. When I made mistakes, I was scared to death, not knowing how I would be viewed, and that led to more mistakes. I was never able to experience the kind of unconditional love that only a mother could give, where you feel like your mother would always be there and would always protect you no matter what. My siblings certainly did their best, but they were at best profoundly loving siblings, not my mother. They were all living far away from where I lived at the time, in search of either a good education or a livelihood. Perhaps things might have been different if my only sister from my mother, Anthonia, who lived in faraway northern Nigeria, could have been around me. I don't know. She too was dealt a heavy blow by the death of our mother, from which she does not seem to have recovered.

All that I know about my mother are stories I heard from those who knew her, including my older siblings and her close friends. One of the most notable stories was how, on the eve of her death, she took me with her and disappeared without letting anyone know where she was going. As it turned out, she took me, her thirteen-month-old baby, and went to a church about a mile away. She had me wrapped around her chest and slept behind the altar until the following morning when she returned to the house. Later that evening, as I was told, she died. It was as though she knew that her end had arrived, so she probably believed that the best thing that she could do for me, her baby, was to go and hand me over to God. Years later, when I became a priest, those who knew that story were quick to make a connection between my priesthood and that last act of apparent entrustment of me to God by my mother.

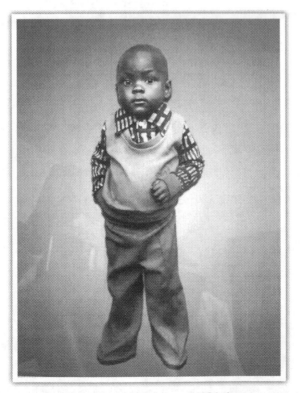

Kingsley growing up in Obike

A Father with a Vision

My father was amazing in his own way. He spared no effort in raising and educating me and the rest of my siblings in a community where more than 90 percent of the citizens were illiterate. Nothing mattered to him more than the education of his children. Thanks to his industry, ten of his children are graduates of some of the best universities in the world. While most of the people in my town were, and many still are, illiterate, my father had already sent one of his sons to study at the prestigious Katolieke Universiteit Leuven in Belgium and was remitting his tuition from our village, Obike, one of the remotest and poorest parts of the world.

He started his career as a teacher and was successful at it. He taught for a mission school where he distinguished himself to a point that would lead to an undesirable consequence. When it came time to choose an outstanding teacher who would be sent to head another school far from our town, he was the inevitable choice. It was indeed like a fulfillment of the old saying that *no good deed goes unpunished*. My father was asked by the missionary priest from Ireland to go to a distant town that had a reputation for cannibalism. Till this day, I cannot say that I know that rumor to be true, but it was one that was widely believed.

When he got news of that assignment, he was quite concerned but somehow convinced himself that he could do it. Yet he had one concern: his mother. When he shared that news with his mother, who was quite aware of the unenviable reputation of this proposed place of assignment, it did not go well. The following morning, after he had communicated his intention to accept this offer, his mother summoned him to her room. As the story was relayed to me, his mother acknowledged his desire to take the risk in search of a better livelihood for his family. However, she was clear in letting him know that she did not approve of it. She gave him a condition that seemed more like finding oneself *between a rock and a hard place*. She told him that if he really wanted to go, he should first perform her funeral and then leave, since she could not bear the thought of him walking into what seemed to her like a lion's den.

My father was her only son, and they shared a very deep bond, so that conversation left him no choice at all. The next morning, he went back to inform the reverend gentleman that he would not be accepting the offer. The priest did not take that too well and did not fail to make it clear to my father that it was an order in which he had no choice. My father told him that he would rather resign than take that assignment against his mother's wishes. The clergyman called his bluff, and he resigned. Knowing how valuable my father was to his mission, the priest rescinded his decision and asked him to stay, but it was too late. My father had already made up his mind to leave. Thus came the end of a teaching career!

As soon as he left the teaching career, he went to get training and certification as a community chemist. In a community of more than twenty-five thousand residents with neither hospital nor any form of medical center, he became a doctor of sorts. He made a name for himself going from village to village providing medical services, and he made a living out of it too. He was excited and quite prepared to move to the next level of becoming the official county medical officer until an unlikely adversary, whose responsibility it was to give the final approval, decided that he would not be appointed to that position. Upset and disappointed, especially given that the individual who denied him this position was a relative, he decided to quit his career as a chemist—the end of another career!

About the same time, a job opportunity was advertised with a company looking to hire migrant workers at a rubber plantation. This company was interested in hiring people with no education at all. All that was required was physical fitness for manual labor. Regardless of his education, he applied and was hired. Soon after, he traveled to Equatorial Guinea in Central Africa, accompanied by my mother and my oldest brother, Leonard. It did not take long for him to stand out from his colleagues. Given his language skills and wit, he was promoted to the rank of an interpreter between his coworkers and their employers. Not long after that, he was appointed the plantation supervisor, responsible for the rest of the workers and accountable to the employers. It brought him both wealth and fame among his colleagues, and five years later, having amassed a significant amount of wealth, he decided to return to Nigeria to open his own business. My brother Chieke was born in Equatorial Guinea, and my mother was pregnant with another brother, Marcellinus, when they returned to Nigeria. Sadly, Marcellinus died in his infancy long before I was born. It was the end of another era and the beginning of a new one!

My father was a dreamer who saw far ahead of his time. He was an entrepreneur quite capable of drawing water out of a rock. As soon as he returned to Nigeria, he revived his trade as an itinerant chemist, combining it with subsistent farming. While this was going on, he spotted an opportunity in sand and gravel excavation from our local stream, *Ogochia*. In order to excel in this business, he traveled to Calabar in Southeastern Nigeria and recruited artisans who were skilled in the business of sand and gravel excavation. He helped them to settle within our community, some with their families, and paid them well enough to be motivated to work for him, while at the same time make a living for himself. Within a short period of time, his business began to thrive. Shortly thereafter, the ugly Nigeria Biafra war broke out. Consequently, my father became an internally displaced war refugee with his unusually large family for the nearly thirty months of that war. All his money in the bank, like those of his fellow Igbo middle class, was seized by the Nigerian government as part of orchestrated economic genocide against the Igbo after the war. He lost everything except, of course, his will, industry, and ingenuity. This was yet another end of an era and the beginning of another!

At the end of the civil war, he started all over again. He went back to his farming and itinerant medicine to provide food for his family and education for his surviving school age children. He would farm extensive land areas by growing cassava, which was processed into *garri,* the staple food, and sold for profit. He was also working to save enough capital to relaunch his prewar sand and gravel excavation business. When he eventually got the business restarted, it brought him so much fortune that he quickly diversified into other businesses. He went into the business of transportation, having purchased lorries, which enabled him to deliver the excavated sand and gravel to buyers and builders. He also purchased pickup trucks to transport local women and men to big town markets like 'Ekeukwu Nnorie, Eke Isu, Afor Enyiogwugwu, and Nkwo Lagwa, among others. It was thanks to these business initiatives that he was able to pay for the education of his children through private colleges and universities within and outside Nigeria.

Dad, Sylvanus and mom, Geraldine

On a Winding Road to a Call …

Growing up, I was so fascinated with the way priests celebrated Mass, and, quite frankly, everything about them. Before anyone knew it, I had littered the walls of my room with all the words that I thought I heard priests say during Mass. I would also role-play by dressing like a priest to celebrate Mass in my room. I did indeed turn my room into a mock church. In my fascination, I began to imagine what it would be like to be a priest. I learned that in order to be accepted into the seminary I needed to first become an altar server. My move to become an altar server also came with its own share of drama. As soon as I applied, someone very familiar with my family, and an altar server himself, confronted me in an effort to assure me that I had no chance of being accepted given that my father was married to more than one wife. This fellow did in fact bring my case up with the executive officers of the altar servers, pressuring them to reject my application. Against all odds, and contrary to his opposition, I got accepted. Two years into my membership as an alter server, I took my entrance exam into the seminary and got accepted to study for the priesthood.

Seminary training was not anything like I had imagined. While I had expected a family atmosphere, where everyone cared for everyone, I found instead what looked more like a military camp, where bullying was the order of the day. The older students maltreated the younger ones in ways that made me wonder whether I was in the wrong place. However, the worst part was that either the authorities saw it as normal or that they were too busy to pay any attention. To me it felt like one of the most hostile environments imaginable. While there was much emphasis on prayer, discipline, and moral formation, and rightly so, it was also an extremely austere environment with plenty of manual labor, sometimes under the intense heat of the sun. Meals were also nothing to write home about. Many of us were so starved that we were always looking for alternative ways to supplement our nutrition. We were not even allowed to bring beverages and snacks to use when we needed them. It was no secret that seminarians would often defy the incomprehensible policy. Yet, to our surprise, the seminary authorities would conduct a search at the beginning of each term in order to seize any snack or beverage that we may have brought back to school. Consequently, we were often hungry. As a result, it became a routine for most of the students to go into the forest each day to pick and crack palm kernels to supplement the inadequate provision of food. I would bet that if the squirrels in those nearby forests could speak, they would have probably confronted us for competing with them for the scarcely available palm fruits and kernels. And coming from my background, having been previously unable to experience a mother's protective love, it was especially excruciating to endure those hardships.

Every first Sunday of the month, we had the opportunity of being visited by our families, and everyone looked forward to it. It was a day when family members socialized, and mothers cooked assorted kinds of food to bring to their children in the seminary. It was simply an extraordinary day. Yet, as you would imagine, with my mother gone, there was not much for me to look forward to on that day. My father never really made out time to visit on those days either. It wasn't that he didn't care. It just wasn't his thing. In effect, what was meant to be a joyful day always ended up being, for me, a very difficult one. Life in the minor seminary, at times, felt quite miserable.

Of all these experiences, I guess it was probably the bullying by older students without much protection from the authorities that hit me the hardest. Before I knew it, I had become quite disillusioned. I was so out of it that I could barely concentrate on my studies and that, unsurprisingly, affected my grades. I began to play truant and would leave the campus without any interest in returning. Before I entered the seminary I was known, at my elementary school, as "the headmaster's boy," thanks to my grades. By the time I graduated elementary school I had won several competitive awards. In my first three years of minor seminary that same boy was unrecognizable. In hindsight, that experience enabled me to appreciate the horror of bullying. By the end of my third year, having seen that I was having a difficult time coping, the rector of the seminary asked me to withdraw, and I did. In an ideal situation, I would have been referred to the services of a school counselor. This was completely unavailable in Nigeria at the time. That is, probably, still the case now. It seemed like the end of a dream.

My struggle with mental health was real. It seemed like I had been able to manage okay prior to my entry into high school. But as soon as I left home to go live in a boarding school, my vulnerabilities were blatantly exposed. I was lonely in a crowd. I cried, I was moody, I was often silent and afraid. As I battled with these difficult emotions, mostly alone, everything began to fall apart. I skipped classes, played truant, and my grades took a heavy hit. Things were so bad that a once honors student could no longer sit through classes without feeling disinterested and bored. I no longer recognized myself. The military style and bully-permissive, atmosphere that prevailed at my Catholic high school (seminary), along with inadequate nutrition, certainly did not help matters. It only exacerbated a latent vulnerability, and became the nail driven through a coffin. I was thrown out of school. It felt, at first, like an unbearable calamity. If there is any doubt that the emotional injuries we bear have enduring ramifications and can change the trajectory of our lives, I am a living proof. Life at that time felt so completely rudderless that that I wondered what meaning there was in it. I felt so alone and lonely in a very crowded world. Life and its challenges were coming so intensely at me that I could not find the time to grieve. Besides, I might have thought it pointless to grieve since no one would have noticed anyway. I felt so invisible. There were times when I would sit in an isolated place wondering what a miserable world. Every time that I saw children and adolescents like me with their mothers, I would imagine what life would feel like to experience that mother-child bond. Yet, imagining was all I could do. I felt such persistent sadness, which today I would describe as clinical depression, that the present seemed unlivable, while the future seemed at best bleak.

When I left the seminary, I thought that nothing worse could possibly happen to me. I took it really hard. Yet, in a surprisingly ironic twist, it turned out to be a blessing in disguise. I switched to a public school, to a much more relaxed type of environment and, sooner than later, the me that I could recognize came alive. But there was also something else. I challenged myself to think about what my life would look like if I imagined myself through my mother's eyes. What if I became the child of her dreams? Who or what would I be? I imagined everything my mother would have desired for me. A woman who brought me to the church and slept behind the altar with me wrapped around her chest, the night before she died. That woman would give me the world if she had it, and would wish for nothing short of the absolute best for me. That question or imagining, and my response to it, was like a key that unlocked it all for me. Almost instantaneously, the cause of my downfall became the source of my rebound. I was able to hope again and to live again. I was able to imagine a future where I would publicly acknowledge, honor, and give credit to my mother through my little and great accomplishments. Everything changed thereafter. From the later part of high school, through college and graduate school, my grades could not have been better. In those years I thrived. Beginning almost immediately with my new high school, I was so completely joyful that soon enough I was able to move on from the prior three years of untold hardships and I started to flourish. In fact, I did so well at that school that I was appointed the Academic Prefect. I was expected to act as a role model, especially, but not limited to matters relating to academics, for the other students. I graduated among the top in my class, ready to go to the university. Each time, I never failed to remember that we did it together, Nda Geraldine and I. (yes, my mother's name was Geraldine, an English name which means "ruler" or "warrior with a spear"). With her spear she has continued to fight along-side me every step of the way. Thus, Nda Geraldine's death, once my stumbling block, became my stepping stone. But she also was my inspiration in another way. Growing up in Obike, I observed women like Geraldine suffer humiliation at the hands of men in a culture that was, and still is in many respects, intolerably chauvinistic. I asked myself if I would allow Geraldine to suffer such dehumanization, and the answer was no. Thus, inspired by her, since each of those women and widows, reminded me of her, I decided that I was going to do something that would honor her someday.

After my disappointing experience while in the minor seminary, one would imagine that I would have no interest whatsoever to return there to pursue a vocation to the priesthood. Yet, as soon as I graduated from my public school, instead of applying to go to the university, like fire in my bones, I continued to experience the urge to return to the seminary to continue my training for the priesthood. Therefore, it was no surprise to me when, instead of applying to go to the university, I applied to return to the seminary. By that time, I had gotten more mature and had developed a tougher skin, better able to cope with adversity. When I eventually went back to apply, the rector who gladly welcomed me, three years later, was the same one who had advised me to withdraw. Today I would definitely recommend a review and restructuring of many aspects of seminary training in Nigeria. Yet, much as I regretted many aspects of those three years in the minor seminary, and the later more mature years in the major seminary, those years taught me lessons in coping with adversity, even if in the roughest of circumstances. They also provided me with a greater sense of appreciation for the sufferings of others.

Born and Raised ...

I was born and raised in Obike, a town of about 25,000 citizens. I was born in a moving vehicle a few miles before the driver could arrive at the health center. Between 85 and 90% of the community was illiterate then and it is still estimated to be mostly so till this day. The very few exceptions included my father who went from being a teacher, to a trained community chemist, then became a self-made entrepreneur.

Earlier, I wrote about how my father managed to break out of the pack to become an incredible entrepreneur, and how he used his resources for the education of his children. But that is only half the story. Besides his investment in his children, my father was also remarkable in his ability to be philanthropic. He was reputed for advocating for the rights of the oppressed, as well as for being an outstanding community organizer. He was one of the highest-ranking members of the king's cabinet, indeed the Palace Secretary, which is comparable to a city council secretary in the United States, but in the scaled-down sense of community. He was also among the king's confidants who were relied upon for important decisions concerning the governance of the community.

Back in the day when communal ownership of property was quite popular, the Obike community started an initiative to send their best and brightest sons to study abroad. To accomplish this magnanimous initiative, the community harvested communally owned palm fruits, processed and sold them for profit in order to raise funds for the education of these young men. As far as I can remember, at least ten men benefited from this initiative and were privileged to be trained in Europe, including Oxford, England. It was a time when, sadly, women were not allowed to compete. The whole idea behind this initiative was to empower these young men so that they would in turn give back to the community. To implement the initiative to support the education of these promising young men, the community grappled with determining who would spearhead the project and, at the same time, designating a trustworthy custodian of the funds. The individual would have the responsibility to remit those funds overseas to these extremely privileged young men. This was at a time when only a handful in that community had any knowledge of such sophisticated financial transactions. It had to be someone with impeccable integrity and of unquestionable character. In the end, the entire community unanimously picked my father for that extraordinary responsibility, and he did not fail them. Led by him, these sons of Obike were educated in some of the best universities in Europe. Many of those individuals, now in their '60s and '70s, have continued to laud my father's huge contributions to their success. Among them are lawyers, doctors, engineers, and educators.

I began this section by stating that I was born in the back seat of a moving car. It is of interest to note that the car in which I was born belonged to one of the men whose education my father helped to sponsor. My brother Chieke sat in the front seat with this gentleman as I came into this world. He was educated in Germany where he became an engineer. The vehicle, a Peugeot 404, was purchased as soon as he returned from Germany after his training. This kind fellow was driving my due-to-deliver mother to the health center when, less than a few miles away, my mother gave birth to me in his vehicle. That incident is the reason that, to this day, many members of my family and friends call me *Nwa Pleasure Car*, which literally translates as "the child of a pleasure car." How surreal it was to be born in the back seat of the vehicle of a man whose education my father championed! God does indeed have a sense of humor. You couldn't find better proof of the fact that *what goes around comes around.*

My father was also involved in a lot of personal philanthropy, materially helping widows and politically advocating for their rights. I watched as he advocated justice on behalf of widows and spent his own resources to feed and support them and their children. Watching many oppressed people, whose causes he pleaded, both in the king's palace and in the customary court, became another enduring source of inspiration for me. Growing up in a patriarchal culture, I witnessed many widows being stripped of their God given rights. The political economy of the community was such that men alone were the locus of rights. Once a woman lost her husband to death, she was often treated as second class, at best. In the distribution of lands, which were mostly communally owned, widows also came last. To this day, land remains the primary source of livelihood, providing most of the people with opportunities for agriculture. Widows were the ones who got the leftovers, or were allocated the plots of land that were the least fertile, after everybody else had been taken care of. Widows were often victimized for the death of their husbands, with no evidence to show for it. In a culture where women struggle to have their voices heard, being a widow added another layer of invisibility to an already odious situation. I observed widows stripped naked by angry kinsmen who sought to scapegoat them for the deaths of their relatives and perhaps also in an effort to dispossess them of any assets or properties left behind by their late husbands. As I painfully and helplessly observed these acts of dehumanization in my youth, coupled with the desire to honor the memory of my mother, the foundation for my ministry to widows was laid. Many notable aspects of these egregious cultural practices have undergone significant revisions, yet vestiges of them remain in significant ways where widows and women in general are denied equal status to men.

Growing up in Obike, there were lots of other kids like me who, due to hardships, had lost one or both of their parents at a very young age. There was one kid in particular whose condition left an indelible impression on my mind, and which became an added motivation for me to act. Sunday lost his mother about the same age as I did. He and I were similar in a lot of ways yet dissimilar in many. Like him, I had no mother, but unlike him, I had a father who could afford to send me to school and pay for my education. For whatever reason, Sunday gravitated toward me and would spend a lot of time with me. By the time I left the village to go to high school, and eventually to the seminary for my priestly formation, he still roamed the village in half-torn clothes and often on an empty stomach. Over time, he developed something that looked like a tumor, which caused his right eye to grow about half the size of his head. It was so large that it looked as though it was going to drop to the ground. Without access to doctors and the privilege of a medical diagnosis, no one knew exactly what it was. Each time I returned home from the seminary, Sunday would come to spend some time with me. And as he left, each time I thought, as Saint Augustine would, "there but for the grace of God goes I." I continued to hope and pray that I could get the resources to at least take him to the hospital so that doctors could diagnose his condition. Hope was all I could do. It never happened. He died at the age of fifteen. Sunday and many kids like him were on my mind as I began my advocacy for widows and orphans. My father too, as I reflected upon his incalculable acts of kindness, especially towards the indigent. But most importantly, my mother whose memory became a catalyst for my rebound. It was in those moments that the seed for a great ministry was sown.

CHAPTER TWO

Be the Change You Desire ...

I at last became a priest in 2003 and was assigned to one of the relatively affluent parishes in Owerri. In this parish, I had a roof over my head, I had food, and all my basic needs met. In addition, I had a Mercedes Benz to drive, not a luxury one, but certainly a functional one which was generously given to me as a gift on my priestly ordination by my family. To top it off, I received a monthly stipend of about $150 dollars. It certainly was a small amount of income in 2003, but all things considered, it was money that I did not need. Having that resource, coupled with generous gifts of money and other material things from my parishioners, I decided that now was the time to be that change which I had always desired. I easily concluded that the best use of the extra funds available to me was to spend it on widows and orphans, beginning with my hometown of Obike. On December 29, 2004, I gathered a group of thirty-five widows and distributed my monthly stipend of $150, which had accumulated over a period of eight months. I also had other food items besides money to offer them on that day. That encounter marked the beginning of the Divine Mercy Ministry. From that month forward, I would go back to Obike every one or two months to distribute money or food items purchased with my monthly stipend. Before I knew it, my parishioners who heard about the beautiful work started to contribute their bit and the generosity started to spread.

Although the amount of money that I gave to them was relatively small, the hope it provided was simply huge. I cannot tell you how many times I was embarrassed as I watched these beautiful women cry tears of joy and gratitude while I shared what little I had with them. A few times when I tried to inquire what was the reason behind their tears, many would tell me that my outreach to them felt like *resurrecting* their hopes, which were all but dead. For three and a half years I continued this beautiful ministry until I was asked by my Bishop to go to Rome for my graduate studies.

Fr. Kingsley with some of the widows before leaving Nigeria for Rome

Leaving Home for Rome ...

Leaving home for Rome was news I received with mixed feelings. On the one hand, I was happy to have been chosen from a large pool of priests to study at the Vatican. I considered that an honor. On the other hand, I was greatly concerned about what was going to happen to these widows once I left home. The thought of leaving them without any help tore my heart to pieces. Yet staying back was not an option. Weeks before I left Nigeria for Rome, I had my last meeting with them at which time I broke the news. Saying goodbye to them was one of the most challenging experiences of my life, as no doubt it was for them as well. I comforted them, promised them my continued support, especially in prayer, while I also requested their prayers on my behalf. On that occasion, they prayed over me and honored me by taking a group photograph with me to keep as a memento of the beautiful experiences we shared.

While in Rome as a student, I had various difficult experiences, including homesickness, my health, the food, the weather, culture shock, and the challenge of studying a difficult discipline in a language that I barely understood. Yet, as difficult as those experiences were, none would compare to the agony of getting frequent calls reporting the deepening woes of the helpless women, many of whom were dying of both curable and preventable diseases. The experience was particularly excruciating because as a student there was not much that I could do to help them. Under the circumstances, the only thing that I could afford was to continue to pray and to hope for a miracle to happen in their favor one way or another.

During those years, I was privileged to meet twice with Pope Benedict. In 2010, I was one of the undersecretaries for the Synod of African Bishops. At the end of that weeklong activity, all the participants were privileged to meet with the Pope. My second encounter with the Holy Father was during that meeting, which lasted approximately fifty-eight seconds. The one topic that I chose to talk to him about was my ministry in Nigeria on behalf of widows. I shared with him how the news of their continued suffering has been a source of sadness to me as I faced my studies in Rome. While I was not hoping for any monetary support from him, I tried to bring to his awareness the sufferings of women in various parts of the world and to request for his prayerful support on their behalf. The Holy Father graciously acknowledged and thanked me for the beautiful ministry and prayed that God may bless and provide support to these women in the following words *"Che il Signore benedica il tuo ministero,"* which means, "May the Lord bless thy ministry." I believed in the efficacy of that blessing and from that moment onward things only got better.

Fr. Kingsley with Pope Benedict XVI

CHAPTER THREE

The Miracle of (Saint Helen) Westfield, New Jersey ...

I n the summer of 2007, I applied to the Archdiocese of Newark, New Jersey, in the United States for a position as a summer substitute clergy. One year later, I received a positive response from the Archdiocese with an assignment at the Catholic community of Saint Helen in Westfield, New Jersey. This notification of assignment came at an unfortunate time. I had just had an operation and was still too fragile to fly seven or eight hours from Europe to America. As a result, I wrote to the pastor of Saint Helen and declined the invitation to work with him. The relentless pastor immediately reached out to me via email in the most gentle but persuasive way, promising that he was going to make sure that my ministry at his parish would be as uncomplicated as possible. In a telephone call with him later, I explained my difficulty considering that I was just fresh from surgery. The monsignor, who would not take no for an answer, smooth-talked me into accepting that assignment, which turned out to be one of the most rewarding assignments of my priestly ministry. As soon as I arrived, Monsignor Harms, of blessed memory, made all the necessary provisions to make my stay enjoyable. First, he went out shopping for me and returned with a bag of clothes, including one bright orange shirt, which he gave to me saying, "I want your life to be brightened." Thereafter, he announced in church that a priest had arrived from Rome to assist him during the summer months of June, July, and August. He also announced that I would need a car to drive around town to procure my needs. He appealed for anyone who had any extra vehicle to spare to please consider lending it to me. That appeal immediately yielded a result as the Gatens, Adele and Gene, donated their vehicle for me to use during the period of my stay at Saint Helen. Gene had recently been advised by his doctor to stop driving which he was having a hard time accepting. His wife Adele and their beautiful daughter, Cathy, were thinking about what best approach to use in convincing Gene to stop driving and follow his doctor's advice. As soon as Monsignor Harms announced that I needed some mobility, the family thought that asking him to donate his vehicle to me would be the best way to wean him off his beloved machine, aware that he would not refuse a priest a favor that he could afford. And it worked. As it turned out Gene, one of the kindest human beings that I have ever known, and I share the same birthday. Gene passed on seven years ago and his beautiful wife Adele passed on in August 2020. May God grant eternal rest to their kind and loving souls.

Perhaps the most consequential experience that I had at Saint Helen was my encounter with the Ehoffs. One Sunday evening as I was unvesting, having celebrated the 6:00 p.m. Mass, this couple, Paula and Clem, came into the sacristy to thank me for a beautiful Mass and to ask if I would consider joining them for dinner.

Fortunately, I had no prior engagement, so I did. We talked about our lives, and I shared stories of my Nigerian origin, my experiences in Rome, and my time at Saint Helen. By the end of that dinner, we had started to feel like we had known each other for a while. Over the course of several meals, which happened almost every weekend while I was at Saint Helen, a bond of friendship was forged. I returned to Rome at the end of that beautiful summer, and we remained in touch. The following year, on another summer assignment, I was assigned to a different parish, in East Orange, New Jersey, about twenty-five miles away from them. Despite the distance, they continued to visit and to attend my weekly masses. On one of those visits, Paula brought her friend Janice and I invited them to spend some time with me at the rectory. As Paula went through my photo album, she was quickly attracted to my photograph with the widows, the very photograph that I had taken with them prior to my trip to Rome. I explained to her the outrageous situation in which these poor widows live and the indignity they suffer. An emotional Paula was so moved by their stories and the efforts that I had made to help them. She told me she thought that what I had done for them was amazing and that she hoped that somehow more people would come to know about the beautiful ministry and to support it. I spoke about my frustration in not being able to assist them any longer and shared my hopes and dreams for the day when I would be able to assist them again like I used to before I left Nigeria. That was where we left things before I travelled back to Rome at the end of the summer of 2009.

Not long after my return to Rome, Paula contacted me to share an unfortunate situation with her daughter who lived in California. Katti had been involved in a very serious sports accident. In a desperate search for a miracle Paula and I started to pray together regularly, including the chaplet of divine mercy. Paula told me that she had no prior knowledge of the power of that prayer. As God would have it, Katti recovered from that accident quite well.

Soon after, Paula contacted me to inform me that she had contacted Kerry, an attorney mutually known to us both, who had agreed to register and incorporate an organization that would promote my ministry to widows and orphans. I received that news with a mixture of surprise and excitement, and before I knew it, Kerry had completed the paperwork. When I was asked about a name with which to register the organization, I told them to use International Widows and Orphans Organization to complete the paperwork. But a few days prior to the submission of the paperwork, I had the most dramatic experience. I woke up suddenly in the middle of the night having had a dream in which I persistently heard a voice telling me that the organization must be named after the "Divine Mercy." I was quite perplexed by the relentlessness of that voice, but more perplexed because everything about the paperwork had already been completed except for submission, which was scheduled to happen in a matter of hours. How could I subject an attorney who was working pro bono to the rigorous task of redoing almost the entire application that took weeks to complete? Yet, I knew by the nature of the message that I could not ignore it. Picking up my phone, I called Paula with the request to have the name changed. She was very surprised to hear that and tried to convince me that we should keep the name as is. By the time I finished explaining to her the circumstances surrounding my decision, she saw no choice but to go along with it. It was not difficult at all to get her husband Clem and Kerry to graciously effect the change before submission. Less than a month after submission, the application was approved and the *Divine Mercy International Widows and Orphans Organization*, hereafter DMIWOO, was registered and incorporated in the State of New Jersey as a 501(c)(3) nonprofit in the United States. In the summer of 2011, with a small group of friends, including the Gatens, my dear friend Judge Sybil Elias and her son Caleb, and the amazing Kathy Dawson, we formally launched DMIWOO at the home of the Ehoffs in Garwood, New Jersey. A dream comes true! It is important to mention that the parish community of Saint Helen has remained among the most generous sponsors of DMIWOO. From the leadership of late Monsignor William Harms, to Bishop Michael Saporito, to Monsignor Thomas Nydegger, the current pastor, our organization has continued to benefit immensely from the generosity of this amazing parish community. Thanks to Paula, we have also received significant support from the priests and parishioners of Most Holy Trinity, a neighboring parish, also in Westfield, New Jersey.

From Small Beginnings ...

With funds raised on the day we launched, we embarked on our initial project as a US-based nonprofit organization: an entrepreneurship training for some of the younger villagers. Obike is a rural community where over 85 to 90% of the population are illiterate farmers. The decision to begin with skills acquisition training addressed our concern of long-term poverty alleviation. Our goal was to empower the people with the knowledge and skills necessary to engage in small businesses with the potential to support themselves and their families rather than enabling them to rely on handouts. I travelled to Obike, our community of interest, to organize the entrepreneurship education. In collaboration with a group of professionals we presented skills acquisition training for the citizens, both men and women. The training attracted over

160 participants including sixty widows. It was a most amazing experience to see so many people, men and women, old and young, so hungry for knowledge yet so deprived. Some of the areas of training that we offered were soap making, poultry farming, sewing, petty-trading and bookkeeping. At the end of the training, twenty widows and young women received grants to start small-scale businesses. Ten years later, a significant number of these businesses are still up and running. While we were able to equip twenty widows, a large majority of those who got trained are still waiting and hoping for their turn to receive funding.

While the skills-acquisitions training targeted the young and able widows, DMIWOO also had great concern for sick and elderly widows without any abilities or means of support. These women had neither an education or any form of skill or any previously held jobs and were mostly left to languish in penury. Therefore, our second project was to provide these impoverished women with grants for food and other basic needs, beginning with the original set of widows on behalf of whom I started the ministry years ago. Today, DMIWOO supports over eighty-five sick and elderly widows.

While my commitment to the well-being of these widows has benefited them tremendously, I must also admit that I have benefited as much and perhaps much more. These widows remind me of my own mother who I did not have the privilege of caring for like she cared for me. So, in each one of them I see my own mother. I wondered if I could have kept silent and watched her suffer such indignities in the same way that these widows have experienced had she been alive? The answer is that I could not. So, they provide me with a most meaningful opportunity to be able to demonstrate, through them, the love that I could not give to my mother. I will continue to be grateful for that.

As a child who grew up without the nurturing presence of a mother, my concern for orphans can hardly be exaggerated. Obike is heavily populated with children who have lost one or both parents due to hunger, disease, or both. The story of my friend Sunday, the orphan who died before I was able to assist him, acted as a huge catalyst to stir me to action. His face was always on my mind, his misery, a constant reminder for me to get to work before more lives, like his, are wasted. To combat the hopelessness of orphans in Obike, DMIWOO initiated a scholarship scheme, the aim of which was to take children out of the streets and send them to schools. We did so out of the conviction that in these children lies the hope of a community. Government "schools" were only so in name. They were characterized by collapsing walls and caved-in and leaking roofs, where most children studied under the shades of trees and sitting on bare floors. We decided that the best place to send these children would be the private schools. Currently DMIWOO has seventy-five children in private schools within Obike and beyond. We also support the care of various children located at three different orphanages, including Ngugo, Uratta, and Emekuku. Each day we are confronted with the need of more children who are no less destitute. Although our resources are limited we continue to embrace a goal to support as many children as possible.

Until 2007, the Obike community of over 25,000 citizens had no access to good drinking water. In that year, four years prior to the incorporation of DMIWOO, a group of professors from Lincoln University in Pennsylvania responded to an appeal from one of their colleagues and my brother Professor Chieke Ihejirika. Thanks to the magnanimity of this group of academics, Ochicha, one of the eight villages in Obike, was generously gifted with a water well that supplies clean water to the surrounding community. It is noteworthy that prior to this huge act of generosity, members of this community relied on water from a local untreated river, where seasonal rains dumped all the refuse and sewage from the community. Since only a handful of people have latrines, the majority would do "their business" in the open, which ended up getting dumped into the same river that they would later draw water from for cooking and drinking. As a result, many contracted all sorts of waterborne diseases, such as river blindness. That was the situation when the Lincoln University group of friends stepped in. What they did was literally lifesaving. Unfortunately, since the community lacked the resources to continue to maintain the facility, it dilapidated and ceased to function as quickly as it was built. DMIWOO stepped in. Not only did DMIWOO revamp the existing water project, but we also contracted labor to expand it. Underground pipes were laid which made water accessible to the entire community. Now our sick and elderly widows and orphans could easily get water, without having to travel long distances to the community center. We also had a generator installed to ensure that the overhead water tank is constantly replenished each time it runs out. Thanks to these efforts the community has access to clean drinking water.

In a community where the average life expectancy is in the low to mid-fifties, it became obvious that in order to bring about any meaningful change we had to improve the health of the people. In 2016, we initiated an annual medical mission project to respond to the health needs of the community. During the first year of this medical mission, we organized a group of medical professionals, both local and from overseas, numbering over 70. Led by the amazing Chioma Acholonu, we set up camps on the premises of the local Catholic church and, working from dawn until dusk, we provided desperately needed medical care to over 3,000 citizens, including non-Obike citizens. Chioma brought her years of experience in medical missions' outreach to bear on the process, in addition to her inimitable passion to promote wellness in rural Nigerian communities. We were shocked to see the level of medical emergencies which would have ended in otherwise preventable deaths. People lacked access to even the most rudimentary kinds of care, such as a temperature and blood pressure check. We encountered cases such as thrush, eczema, canker sores, malnutrition, shingles, dry and wet cough, pneumonia, acute diarrhea, typhoid, arthritis, excessively high blood pressure, diabetes and diabetic wounds left untreated, terrible heart diseases, and more. Among the babies and infants below the age of three, there were a lot of bacterial infections on different parts of their bodies and very many were hypoglycemic. There were also people who were basically suffering from a lack of proper hygiene, reminding us to make education for basic hygiene an important component of our mission. By the end of this first weeklong program, we had provided care to an enormous number of people, many of whom could have died otherwise. Nevertheless, there were still many more who could not be seen either because we ran out of time or out of supplies. Those who could not be seen were so disappointed because it would take one whole year, if we came back for another visit, for them to get another opportunity— assuming they made it through the year.

The subsequent years of medical mission trips were no different except that the number of people to be seen continued to grow exponentially, given that more people had become aware of the services we provided. In fact, in the second year, we had to extend our medical services beyond Obike to Obokwe, one of the neighboring towns. Word had spread and we had patients from within a twenty-mile radius of Obike coming to receive free treatment. They would not be able to get or afford access to medical care in any other way.

An additional reason that the people had confidence in the quality of service we provided was because 95% of all the medications we administered were shipped from the United States. It was particularly important for the people to have faith in the credibility of the drugs being administered because such faith was lacking in their own care system and in the quality of the drugs that were available to them. Being able to get access to products that they could trust meant a lot to them.

After several medical mission experiences with growing needs, we concluded that a once-a-year medical mission would not be enough to cater to the monstrous health needs of the community. That realization led us to consider building a medical facility where people could have access to quality health care on a more regular basis.

We were compelled by other factors as well, including that one in five children in Obike died before the age of five, there is a one in thirteen chance that a woman will die in pregnancy or childbirth, only one in six women receive prenatal care, two-thirds of births occur in private homes leading to complications that often end in preventable deaths, and only 68% of pregnant women receive iron supplements. Only 39% of the people receive treatment for malaria, which is the chief cause of infant mortality. Sadly, Nigeria has the highest mortality rate of children under five in Africa and the second highest worldwide. All factors considered, the decision to move forward and build a medical facility was made.

Our visit to one of the 3 orphanages that we support

The Good People of the Sacred Heart Parish ...

The Sacred Heart Church in Oxford, Pennsylvania, is home to my brother Chieke, his wife Anno, and my four amazing nephews and nieces. From spending my holidays with my family, I developed a relationship with the pastor, Fr. Gregory Hamil, who had had a previous pastoral experience in Ethiopia. His experience in Africa certainly helped to put things in perspective for him as far as the sufferings of people in other parts of the developing world. Fr. Hamil became aware of our work to support widows and orphans through my conversations with him and those he had with Prof. Chieke. In his compassion, he gave instruction that the parish weekly poor box, which was their facility for helping those in need, be designated exclusively to the support of our ministry. He also extended an invitation to me to speak to the entire parish about the DMIWOO mission and vision. It has been about eight years since that presentation at the Sacred Heart church, yet members of that church continue to be some of the major supporters of our work.

During my annual visit to the Sacred Heart church in 2016, which was usually to thank them for their support and to give an update concerning our efforts, I decided to share our medical mission experiences and the need to provide better access to medical care without further delay. That presentation was received with very generous contributions from parishioners and very kind words of encouragement. Even after I left, parishioners continued to call me and to ask how they could help.

CHAPTER FOUR

A Most Extraordinary Parish (MHT Wallingford)

I n January 2017, I was assigned to the Most Holy Trinity in Wallingford, Connecticut. By almost every measure, my experience serving at Most Holy Trinity parish was phenomenal. I had an amazing pastor and incredibly supportive parishioners. Life was good. About seven months into our partnership, this pastor was transferred and replaced by a younger priest. The transition went smoothly. We partnered well and got many compliments from the parishioners. We ate together as often as possible and discussed matters relating to parish administration as frequently as the need arose. During one of our conversations, I spoke to him about DMIWOO. He was so impressed, and he invited me to also speak to the parish council about it. I was grateful for his generosity and accepted his invitation to speak about it at the next parish council meeting. My message was well received beyond my imagination. Some members of the council who were present spoke about how it reminded them of a prior overseas mission to Africa that they had supported, and how it would provide the opportunity for another international ministry. The pastor and council decided that a date should be determined for when I could speak to the larger parish population about it.

As providence would have it, the priest who was scheduled to speak on Mission Sunday called to postpone his visit and the pastor decided that it would be the perfect day to speak about DMIWOO. I spoke at all four masses that weekend. In my speech, I chronicled the history of DMIWOO as a nonprofit organization and why the need for a medical facility had become so urgent. It was the most enthusiastic and most generous response to a request that one could imagine. Before the middle of the week, over forty people had responded to my request to serve as members of a committee that would look into raising funds for the construction of a medical facility. By the time the committee gathered for its inaugural meeting, at the dining room of Most Holy Trinity rectory, we could barely find enough room to accommodate all those who had come to serve. Because I had previously shared with a couple of friends from among the group what the budgeted cost for the construction of the facility would be, some came with clearly drafted plans of how we could meet that goal sooner than later. Since the space at the rectory was barely enough to accommodate everyone, people offered their larger office spaces for weekly meetings of the group. It was the most uplifting experience imaginable. The amount of enthusiasm in support of the project was sky high. Not only did many people respond to my request to serve as volunteers, but others also responded by making contributions toward the building of the medical facility, and still others reached out to me either by telephone call or email, thanking me for what they saw as an amazing ministry, and for providing them with a wonderful opportunity to reach out to those in need.

These were people that I had already formed a bond with. They were an enthusiastic and philanthropic Christian community. They knew me and I knew and served them daily. I believe that their generosity and willingness to support this international mission was reinforced by the fact that they were hearing about it directly from me, its founder, and by knowing that I was directly involved in the decision-making and management of the organization. By the time I left for Nigeria that December, we had raised quite a significant amount of money in support of the medical facility. My parish life and my mission calling were all coming together and progressing seamlessly. Together we were professing and living the gospel values that we believed. It was a blessed time.

In January, I returned from Nigeria to find that allegations had been made that the activities of DMIWOO were causing division within the parish. It was quite shocking considering that, prior to my trip, there was palpable enthusiasm in support of this ministry, along with a great outpouring of love and support. The concern was that asking parishioners to support DMIWOO would somehow stop them from supporting the local parish. Unfortunately, at that time there were no written guidelines for nonprofits that could be followed. The situation was cause for great mental and emotional distress, both for me and for so many concerned parishioners. Tension, anxiety, name-calling, and mischaracterizations ensued. I was truly saddened and felt quite hurt that what started as a labor of love had become needlessly controversial.

I answered questions about the legal status of DMIWOO, the management of funds, the board and the beneficiaries. As DMIWOO was founded and has always been run legitimately, following all US guidelines for a 501(c)(3) nonprofit, all information was public and readily available. The background and history, as well as the mechanics of the organization— including the need for the medical facility— were reviewed. The fact that the decision to share this project with the parish on Mission Sunday had come about through collaborative conversation with, and at the invitation of, the current pastor and parish council was also discussed. Yet, because of the controversy and as a precautionary measure, information concerning the organization was no longer shared in any parish media, bulletins or announcements. Events were still held outside the parish and parishioners were all still welcome to participate.

People became concerned, and many reached out to ask me why they were no longer getting updates and information about the Divine Mercy project. It appeared the fire that had been ignited was being extinguished. It did not make sense that the same parishioners who called me, sent emails, stood up and applauded, came personally to thank me for providing them with the opportunity to assist a community in need would turn around to call and complain that my organization was creating division within the parish. Not long after, I was transferred to a different parish where I became the administrator. My pastor at Most Holy Trinity was also transferred to a different parish to serve elsewhere.

As difficult as the situation was, it did not discourage the beautiful people of Most Holy Trinity parish, nor DMIWOO and its supporters, from wading through the obstacles to reach our goal. In fact, that experience might have actually provided added motivation for people to continue relentlessly to ensure that the project was completed. Through these excruciating times, I had the most amazing parishioners and friends to rely upon. My bosom friend Fr.

Emmanuel Ihemedu, through whose recommendation I joined the archdiocese of Hartford, was, as always, a fortress of support.

Now, having taken time to process that entire experience, I have made the decision to let go of any hurt feelings, knowing that to continue to nurture those feelings would be entirely unhealthy. And, although I may not ever know or understand the reasons behind the unfortunate controversy, I bear no one ill will. I also appeal to anyone who may have felt hurt or betrayed by what happened to please let go. There is a tremendous healing power in forgiveness. And what we do not often realize, to quote Lewis B. Smedes, is that: *to forgive is to set a prisoner free and then to realize that the prisoner was you.* I have been blessed in innumerable ways. Holding grudges would be nothing short of ingratitude to God who has been infinitely gracious to me. Always remember that when you hold grudges, your hands are not free to catch blessings. One of the beneficial lessons I took away from that traumatizing experience is that, as Nicole Reed reminds us: *there is a way in which some of the worst things that happen in our lives can open the way for some of the best things that could possibly happen.*

An Extremely Rapid Response …

First, the Reinmanns, Tom and Laurie, who owned a car garage, came up with the idea of a car wash. The entire Most Holy Trinity church community, as well as the Most Holy Trinity school kids were involved. Spearheaded by the Reinmanns, and other amazing friends like Sue Hair and Sharon Healey, we were able to realize over $3,000 just from washing cars. According to Tom, it was the most amount of money that he had ever raised from that type of fundraiser, which he had done quite a few times in the past. Even those who did not need their cars to be washed made donations while others brought their very clean vehicles to be rewashed just for the fun of it, and just so they could contribute.

As success leads to success, the same Most Holy Trinity community of parishioners, led by Tom and Laurie, Sue Hair, Sharon Healey, Bob and Mary Hughes, Kim and George Marinelli, and Christine and Marty Mansfield, organized a Christmas cookie sale. Even people who had never baked cookies volunteered to do so just to support the cause. My dear friend Karen Grasser of blessed memory, who was struggling with a life-threatening illness at the time, would not allow her condition to deny her the opportunity to be a part of this history-making event. She too arranged to make her own cookies, joined by another dear friend Mary Hughes, her sister Kathleen, and yours truly. Tom Grasser, her husband and my friend, was also available to lend a helping hand where necessary. In that same year, Karen requested her three children to donate toward the building of the medical facility in lieu of a Christmas gift for her, and they were very glad to do so. Another group of friends, Sue and Lori, invited me to join them in baking cookies as well, and I was delighted to do so. The day of the sale turned out to be quite an amazing experience. Even those who had not originally indicated interest in baking cookies ended up doing so, while those who could not bake purchased already made cookies to be resold. It was another record setting event as we realized over $2,300 from the sale.

Following that effort, the Divine Mercy medical clinic group of volunteers, in collaboration with the Most Holy Trinity parish "Mission Possible" group, organized another fundraiser. Mission Possible is an incredible parish ministry whose mission is to assist struggling communities with all kinds of services, including the repair of dilapidated schools and residential homes, on an annual basis. Upon hearing about the DMIWOO clinic project, members of this amazing group were immediately taken by the idea of building a medical facility in the rural community of Obike. As a result, they decided to join with us in a fundraiser that would support their efforts locally in the United States, and at the same time contribute toward the building of this desperately needed medical facility. Once again, all hands were on deck. By the time I returned from my trip to Nigeria in January of that year, a member of the committee had made and donated several wine glasses, on which had the inscriptions of the two focus projects, to be sold at the fundraising event. George and Kim Marinelli, two passionate supporters of the effort to build a medical clinic, in collaboration with some committee members, had produced and single-handedly paid for a brochure which served as a case statement for the proposed medical facility. That document, which was handed out at the fundraising event, became one of the single most important advertisements for the medical facility.

Laurie Reinmann went out of her way to convince a travel agency to donate vacation packages, including flight and hotel accommodation, which became money spinners for the fundraiser. Daniela and David Tristine, an incredibly generous couple and owners of a wine shop, provided all the wine for the event. They also took time to decorate the hall. God bless them.

Members of the group knocked on every door soliciting for funds and for gift baskets that would be sold during a silent auction. I arranged for Nigerian fabrics, outfits, and artworks to be brought over from Africa and sold at the event. We had friends and family join us from the northeastern part of the United States and beyond, while others joined us from Nigeria. In the end we raised over $20,000 split between Mission Possible and the Divine Mercy medical facility project, from nearly 250 people who had gathered for the event. The

Mission Possible team, that had previously organized a number of fundraisers for their annual mission projects, noted that this combined fundraiser with DMIWOO was by far the most successful fundraiser that they had ever organized.

In their relentless commitment to the medical facility project, the Reinmanns came up with another fundraising idea, a rummage sale. Friends and members of the community were invited to collect new and used items which would be sold to raise funds. Like the fundraisers before that, the level of enthusiasm and participation was out of this world. Tom Reinmann, who championed this effort, could not keep up with people calling him to come pick up donated items from their homes. There were all kinds of items; from bicycles, to exercise equipment, to books and artifacts. Tom and Laurie even pledged to donate a percentage of the proceeds from the sale of their store of antiques in support of the medical facility. As it turned out, that day ended up rainy and cold. Yet, none of that would deter hands and hearts so full of warmth for a people they have only heard about. Under a freezing temperature, our incredibly generous committee members like Bob and Mary Hughes, Sharon Healy, Sue Hair, Maureen Socha Cruz, Cyndi Johnson, Joyce Gomez, Dan Gilhuly, Elena and Armido Pires, Bruno and Diane Pereira, and Ellen Paiva showed up to help. That effort again raised over $4,000. Just as we were rejoicing over such a huge success, the Healeys' pledged to match that amount thereby doubling it to over $8,000 in another incredibly successful effort.

Volunteers after our Rummage Sale

In the fall of 2018, having joined me on a mission trip to Obike earlier in the year, which she described as lifesaving, Kim Marinelli and her husband George led the organization in a comedy night fundraiser. This event again brought together a coalition of volunteers and donors preparing gift baskets and other donated auction items. We also had more vacation packages to auction, thanks to the infinite and generous connections of Laurie Reinmann. Committee members reached out to their friends who in turn reached out to other friends.

The highlight of the occasion was the personal testimonies of experiences from the four patrons of DMIWOO who had travelled with me to Nigeria in the late summer of that same year. Proudly exhibiting their chieftaincy regalia, Phil, Bob, Joe, and Kim spoke of their experiences, including the suffering, the corruption, the chaos, the warmth, and yes, the kindness of the people they met in Nigeria and Obike. That experience convinced them about the urgency of the project while motivating them to appeal to others for support. The event brought in another $10,000.

Prior to that trip to Nigeria, George and Kim had initiated a weekly bingo that would continue to generate funds for the completion of the project. Several volunteers, including Sharon Healey, Sue Hair, Lori Moutinho, Karen Brown, Bronwen Wrinn, Cinde Lector, Joyce Gomez, Bob and Mary Hughes, Melanie Petote, Sylvia and Richie Porylo, Kate Boyd, and Armido Pires volunteered to support the weekly event. Each week, we had over a hundred seniors and others who gathered to play. I would drive from Hartford to Wallingford to speak to the players concerning our goal for the fundraiser and to support the volunteers in whatever ways that I could. It was such fun to see so many people, like my dear friend Bob Hajnal, gather not just to win money but to support a cause they each considered worthy. But much more so, I was amazed at the dedication of the volunteers who would drive straight from work to help at the event every Monday night. For the many weeks that it lasted, bingo events raised a significant amount of money for the building of the medical clinic, in another show of incredibly self-sacrificial commitment by the volunteers to the welfare of people in need. Indeed, George and Kim, former board members, had become some of the most dependable champions of the DMIWOO project. They accompanied me to New Jersey to address the Rotary Club of

Westfield, to the Sacred Heart Church in Oxford, Pennsylvania, and to Quinnipiac University to do the coin toss at a fundraising rugby match to support our medical facility. George literally created an office space in his house that was dedicated to anything related to DMIWOO, besides going about talking to everyone about our beautiful mission. The remarkable accomplishments of DMIWOO owe a lot to their unflinching commitment to our mission, and I owe them my deepest gratitude.

In the winter of that same year, Laurie and Tom organized a trip to the Mohegan Sun Casino with a group of about fifteen people. It was a fun day that brought together a coalition of like-minded people united for a good cause. We all met at a central location where we took off to the casino. For lunch, we dined at the legendary Mohegan Sun buffet which provided an opportunity to make further connections with each other. From the sale of tickets and other promotional items, we raised a little over $1,000 to add to the pot.

On October 5, 2019, the feast day of Saint Faustina, the Divine Mercy visioner, Laurie Reinmann led a team of spirited volunteers in another incredibly successful wine tasting event. Laurie was assisted by Sharon Healey, Doreen Gilhuly, Sue Hair, Maureen Socha Cruz, Bronwen Wrinn, Jill Barrett, Judith Williams, Cinde Lector, Claire Portier, Karen Mazurek, Cleveland Horton, Ellen Paiva, Beth Ranchinsky, Cheryl Lawrence, Donna Shears and Sandie Sammarco, Monique Grey, Idalis Ramos, and Elma Ramos. The event was hosted at the Knights of Columbus Lodge in Hamden, Connecticut, and the Healeys, whose generosity towards the DMIWOO project could hardly be matched by anyone, paid the fee for the event venue. As with previous fundraisers, volunteers donated generous baskets for silent auction. The amazing Bron, one of our most enthusiastic volunteers, had more artworks to be sold at the event than I have ever seen. There were also vacation tickets to be auctioned, thanks, once again, to the industry of Laurie Reinmann. It was another extraordinary gathering of good people for a good cause, as the beautiful Katie Reinmann, Tom and Laurie's second daughter, debuted as the master of ceremony. My dear friend and irreplaceable organist, Mark Neumann, coupled with the incredibly talented Heather O'Connor, were on hand to perform. In addition to friends from Wallingford, there was also a significant representation of my friends and parishioners from Saint Justin-Saint Michael parish in Hartford. Laurie, Kay Taylor-Brooks, and Melanie Petote collaborated to work on an event brochure in which several friends posted goodwill messages which helped to bring in additional revenue. Lisa Katz of Amity Wine and Spirits graciously provided all the wine for tasting at the event. By the end of the event, we had raised a whopping $23,000. Another huge success.

Another outstanding supporter of the DMIWOO project is my friend Tom Dacey. Tom started by giving publicity to our work on his weekly live Facebook show "Talking with Tom," where he had me and the Reinmanns' come to promote one of our fundraisers. Since then, Tom has organized two separate fundraisers including one for his annual Tommy Papalooza and another for his birthday. Between these fundraisers, Tom has raised over $3,000 in support of our medical facility project. For his annual fundraiser organized for DMIWOO, Tom knocked on the door of nearly every business owner in the city of Wallingford and he made sure to go back, after the event, to thank them all personally. It is noteworthy that Tom was born with a disability that has kept him in a wheelchair his whole life. Yet, he has remained one of the most sunny-hearted, positive-minded, and extremely generous people that I know. Tom's attitude is a lesson in relentless optimism and in knowing, as they say, that *your background must not keep your back to the ground.* Many members of the Dacey family have become supporters of the DMIWOO project thanks to Tom. Ellen Paiva is another dear friend who has also made a significant contribution to the DMIWOO project. After watching the video of our orphans, where they played soccer with no shoes on, Ellen was moved to start a campaign to collect soccer equipment from various organizations and individuals. Ellen also collected educational materials to benefit our orphans. DMIWOO is deeply grateful to Ellen, her family and friends, for their very generous efforts.

Daniel Healey, Fr. Kingsley and Tom Dacey

From the Mouths of Babes ...

Prior to any of the above fundraisers, I received the most beautiful surprise. One Sunday, immediately after Mass, having returned from Nigeria to the United States from my Christmas vacation, a five-year-old came to present me with a surprise of my life. It was a testament to the power of social media. While in Nigeria, I had posted pictures on Facebook so that friends could see our visits to the orphanages and the schools where our orphans were enrolled. It happened that the O'Hala's, Teresia and Gary, were among those who saw my Facebook posts, and fortunately, their cute little grandson, Bo, was with them at the time. On seeing those pictures of children like him, Bo, who is probably one of the most curious-minded kids that I have ever known, asked his grandma to explain to him what it was that we were doing with those children. On learning that they were orphans and what that meant, Bo made a decision that, for a five-year-old, would remain a shock to anyone. He decided to give away his entire savings to feed these kids. When he heard that I had returned to the United States, Bo came with his grandparents, Teresia and Gary, accompanied by his beautiful little sister Reese, and his parents, Rob and Kathlyn, to donate all the money that he had in his piggy bank to "Fr. Kingsley's orphans." As Bo emptied his entire piggy bank, on that beautiful Sunday morning, he instructed me precisely to use his money to feed the kids. The emotions that I felt in that moment were simply indescribable. This little boy was nothing short of an angel in human form. Ever since, Bo has made it the task of his life to continue to raise money for the orphans. About the same time that he made the donation, Bo drew a picture of himself with very elongated hands which, as he explained it to me, represents him trying to reach out to the children in Nigeria. Bo's thoughtfulness towards impoverished children was so remarkable that News 5 television reported it in one of their evening segments as a human-interest story. This little boy's inimitable kindness brought so much publicity to our work. Subsequent to that, the Record Journal newspapers, thanks to the efforts of Laurie and Tom Reinmann, wrote another story to help publicize the work that we do. Not too long ago, Bo stopped by, accompanied by his amazing grandma, Teresia, to bring me another heavy bag of money which he challenged his family to collect over the course of one year. Bo convinced his entire family— mom, dad and sister, grandma and grandpa, as well as his uncle who lives in Arizona— to keep collecting money so he can continue to help his friends in Nigeria. On his visit to deliver this gift jar, as he called it, he had a number of questions for me. Namely, how much are the people in Nigeria affected by the COVID-19 pandemic? Will the people in Nigeria be able to have access to the vaccine? And the sweetest of all was: "You said that there will be a children's unit at the hospital, is that still the plan?" I told him that, of course, it is still the plan, and we will proudly have your name somewhere on the walls in that unit. It made him so very happy, and I could see a certain sense of accomplishment shine through his little eyes. Bo is simply one of a kind.

Other kids have also supported our efforts to educate children like themselves. Another amazing little boy and my friend, Kaden Barrett, has twice organized fundraisers with the help of his most amiable mom, Jill, to help with the construction of our medical facility. Kaden also reaches out to his friends to make sure that they are collaborators with him in this amazing mission. Every time that he delivers his hard-earned checks, and sometimes cash, to me, he wants to know how many bricks that his contributions can purchase and how soon people can begin to receive care from the facility.

Kaden has done these fundraisers with dedication that could inspire even the most unrepentant skeptic. Besides their passionate support for DMIWOO, Jill and Kaden have also been tremendous sources of support for me personally in my ministry. Jill has shown me the kind of availability that only a loving sister could provide, which is why I am proud to call her my "sister" from a different mother. Despite having been through very significant challenges in her life, Jill's courage in the face of adversity and her compassion for the sufferings of others fill me with daily inspiration. My prayers and blessings will forever be with them both. Also, a group of little children from the CCD class of Most Holy Trinity, organized by the amazing Maria Avila, donated jars filled with money to support our work. It's hard to exaggerate the significance of these donations from these little angels, reaching out to other kids like themselves in a phenomenal show of solidarity.

Interest in this project was astounding across the board. Even college students saw the value in contributing to the DMIWOO ministry, and they would not miss a chance to be a part of it. With huge help from the incredible Monique Drucker who, at the time, was a vice president at the prestigious Quinnipiac University in Hamden, Connecticut, and assisted by their chaplain, Fr. Jordan, the students organized a rugby match raising over $3,000 to support the building of the medical facility. Many of them at the time entertained thoughts of a trip to Obike to visit and interact with members of the community, as well as volunteer their services at the medical facility.

Fr. Kingsley with Bo and little sister Reese

Kaden and buddy George

Four Extraordinary People— Two Ladies and Two Gentlemen

Most Holy Trinity parish was also significant to me for another reason. When I was first assigned to serve in this parish I was hesitant, having been previously given the wrong impression about the pastor. Armed with that information, I went back to the Vicar for Clergy to ask if he could assign me elsewhere. When I shared with him my concerns about the priest as the reason behind my decision, a surprised Vicar encouraged me to go and chat with the priest first, bring up my concerns with him, and hear what he had to say before making up my mind. I did as he advised, went to the priest and shared with him all my concerns about him. Like a truly wise and experienced priest, he encouraged me not to make my decision based on hearsay, but instead to try working with him so I can separate for myself truth from falsehood. As it turned out, this priest was one of the kindest, most caring human beings that I had worked with. I made him aware of my health challenges from the beginning and from that moment on, no day passed without him asking about my health and well-being. The real person that I worked with was nothing like the things that had been said about him. He was a perfect gentleman, very respectful of me as a person and priest, and quite appreciative of my efforts. That experience was another lesson in the fact that we should not judge a book by its cover. Unfortunately, my stay with him was short-lived as he was transferred to another parish only seven months later, and that marked the beginning of a different kind of experience.

As soon as I arrived in the parish God sent me a special woman. One of a kind, Sue Hair, an angel in human form. Without knowing my previous history or background, and without minding my race or ethnicity, a person of African descent in a community of persons of Caucasian descent, Sue took me in like her own child. The love that shone through her looks and expressions was so genuine and so sincere. I could very easily call her mother, despite our ethnicities, because that was the first time that I experienced a love so profound and so kind. Sue was completely available with her services and prayerful support. I trusted her so completely because she loved me so unconditionally. When I had any good news, she was the first one with whom I thought to share it, but when I had a not so pleasant experience, I dreaded to tell her, knowing how much it would break her heart. Again, I could call her my mother, because her attitude toward me reflected nothing less. She made me feel completely at home. It has been nearly three years since I left Most Holy Trinity parish, yet I wake up every morning to a message from Sue: "God bless you Fr." Sue is indeed an inspiring reflection of love in its kindest and truest sense. God bless her.

Fr Kingsley with Sue, Pauline and Lorraine

There was also another Godsend, Betty Hunt and her husband Kevin. Betty and Kevin had both retired, one as a therapist, the other as an allergy doctor who trained at the famous Johns Hopkins Hospital in Maryland. My first conversation with this couple happened at a parish event that took place in the church basement. Upon learning that I was Nigerian, Betty and Kevin became very excited to tell me about an amazing encounter they had with a Nigerian student and priest who was studying in Italy at a time when they were visiting that country. As tourists in Italy, Betty and Kevin had had a problem with finding the right train that would take them to their destination. Suddenly, out of nowhere, emerged this good Nigerian who put himself at their service until they arrived safely at their destination. That experience left a lasting impact on them. They had since invited that Nigerian priest to their house in the United States, making sure to take him to eat the most delicious lobster in town as a token of their appreciation. Apparently, their encounter with me reminded them of this kind gentleman. I was benefiting from someone else's good behavior, in the same way that we sometimes suffer from the indiscretions of other people.

My second encounter with Betty and Kevin took place at a parish event where I had been invited to speak to the Trinity Ladies Club. As the new kid on the block, this socioreligious group of parishioners invited me to speak to them as a way of introducing myself to them and vice versa. In that speech I shared my life's journeys from Nigeria to Rome and to the United States. And since my health challenges have been such an integral part of who I am, I decided to share those as well. I spoke about the numerous surgeries that I had over a very short period, as well as the associated challenges and impact on my diet and lifestyle. While I spoke to the group, and unbeknownst to me, Kevin, who was a well-known and respected doctor, took careful notes of what I had been through. As it turned out, Kevin was very conversant with my health condition and well aware of how it could be managed. At the end of the presentation, many of the people present, including Kevin and Betty, came to thank me for being so vulnerable in sharing such details about my life. Afterward, Betty and Kevin invited me over for dinner at their house. It was during the course of that dinner that Betty informed me that she and Kevin had decided to take care of my meals every day for the entire duration of my ministry in their parish no matter how long it lasted. It was hard to believe that anyone could be so generous to someone that they barely knew. I wondered what may have caused them to act so extremely gracious toward me. Perhaps their experience with the Nigerian who helped them in Italy played a role, or perhaps that's just who they are. Or perhaps it was a combination of both. Either way, it was simply extraordinary. They were genuinely concerned for my well-being. Over the course of several months both Betty and Kevin continued to live true to that commitment. Kevin would spend hours on the computer researching any given food that they were going to prepare for me, and Betty took so much care to make sure they were made to my taste. The best part was that they did not cook just anything. Betty would send me a list of options each day to choose from and even invite me to come up with food of my choice outside of her list. Many times, I would arrive late to eat my meals, due to pastoral exigencies, and this incredibly kind couple would wait patiently for me to come and have my meal. Betty and Kevin never left town without making adequate provision for my meals. In fact, on one occasion, as they were leaving for Florida where they would normally escape during the winter months, Betty reached out to seven different women from the parish who she trusted, and assigned each one of them one day of the week when they were required to cook for me. And since Betty does not like to leave loose ends, she made sure to provide each of these women with recipes and directions on how to prepare my meals and, in some cases, she even purchased and delivered the ingredients, sometimes against the wishes of those individuals, just to make sure nothing was overlooked. I do not think that love could be more loving. And yet, this was the very parish that I was reluctant to go to and serve.

CHAPTER FIVE

The Board Decides ...

The DMIWOO is comprised of a board of eleven seasoned professionals under my leadership. This board of extraordinarily gifted individuals has a fiduciary responsibility to ensure that we do not derail from the founding mission and vision of the organization. Their vote is always critical to the initiation of any project. Convincing the board to take on the building of a medical facility was a bit of an uphill task. There was fear of undertaking too many back-breaking tasks at a time. Some wondered how a medical facility would square up with our original goal of simply supporting widows and orphans. With open-minded, and sometimes heated conversations, we were able to arrive at the conclusion that good health for all members of the community was the most solid foundation upon which we could build anything of lasting value for the widows and orphans that we serve. A sick widow, who is unable to eat due to illness, would not find any use for a food grant; just as an unhealthy orphan could hardly think about education. In other words, as the old African saying goes, health is wealth. Once the board saw the need they went all in and that's what is amazing about our group of board members and volunteers. From that moment onward, the board started to develop all kinds of strategies that would help deliver this desperately needed facility to the community. It has been my experience that as soon as our DMIWOO board becomes sure that any project is worth fighting for, their cautious skepticism often gives way to unmatched enthusiasm with each one working together toward the same goal.

DMIWOO 2021 Board of Directors

Paula Ehoff

Clem Ehoff

Father Kingsley Ihejirika

Chieke Ihejirika

Annette Reyman

Emmanuel Ihejirika

Bob Hughes

Mary Hughes

Kathy Dawson

Marcia Meehan

A Grateful Community Responds ...

On January 2, 2016, I returned to Obike to announce to the community our plan to build a medical facility. The level of excitement from that news was immeasurable. More than 85% of the population were willing to immediately point to a piece of land where we would build. However, there were a handful of skeptics who didn't think that giving up a community-owned land in exchange for a clinic was a good idea. For a long time, they had explained, different people had promised to provide the community with such basic amenities, but those promises were never kept. So, to many, my promise sounded like the same old unkept promises. To address these concerns, we held a series of meetings with members of the community, including men, women, and youths. The youth in particular understood the significance of the project, so they made sure that healthy skepticism did not get in the way of an enormously life-changing opportunity. Women's groups also played an important role in helping the men see the opportunities inherent in my proposal.

The Igbo society is a complicated political system which combines both the hierarchical preeminence of an elder statesman, and the collective will of the population in the decision-making process. Through numerous conversations, led by the community head, the people were able to conclude that donating a piece of land for the construction of a medical facility would be in their best interest, despite dissenting voices. Yet, none of that came without first explaining to them how much stake they would have in the project. The decision to proceed with the donation of land for the facility did not quench the dissenting voices who continued their opposition.

To be clear, those who were skeptical had good reasons to do so. First, there had been previous failed promises, as I noted earlier, so *once bitten twice shy*. Besides, for a community that relied almost entirely on agriculture, and in the absence of any other sources of revenue, a piece of land to them was worth a gold mine; it was clearly the only valuable asset they possessed. In order to give up such an asset of inestimable value, it made sense that they would be asking to know what they would be getting in exchange. Despite my best efforts to explain it to them, that small minority group remained doubtful. Yet, once the majority had agreed to proceed, that group could no longer hold us back. The community showed me quite a few pieces of land, giving me the option to pick any one of them. And while I had requested for just enough space for the medical facility, they generously offered much more in hope that more than just a medical facility could also one day be located there. So, they were hopeful and forward thinking. The community requested to be paid some compensation for trees with economic value that would be removed in the process of construction, and DMIWOO was very pleased to do that. I also provided extra compensation to the community to cushion the effect of the removal of such a valuable asset from them.

As soon as we were able to get past all the hurdles of land acquisition and clearing, we commenced the immediate walling of the complex without further delay. In a matter of a couple of weeks we were able to set up a perimeter wall of over nine feet in height around the entire property to protect it from trespassers. By the time I left Nigeria at the end of January 2016, we had walled and gated the entire land designated for the construction of our medical facility. Perhaps one of the most remarkable things that happened was that two young men, whose parents were strongly opposed to the donation of the land for the medical facility, came to ask to be hired as masons when work started. Without thinking twice, I instructed that they be hired. They helped to erect the walls and got paid for it. One great lesson to learn from that experience is that *"in a world where we can be anything, it is always best that we choose to be kind."*

Emeañaa, a Man with a Mission ...

I returned to the United States after that trip with a huge sense of accomplishment. I was excited to share the details of my trip with my friends and parishioners. But the joy of that experience was short-lived. Less than one month after my return, I received a call in the middle of the day that Emeañaa had died. Emeañaa was the leading voice in convincing the reluctant members of the community. Not only that, he also went all over the village trying to convince everybody not to miss this wonderful opportunity. In effect he acted like a gadfly, urging the community to make a thoughtful decision. Emeañaa was a peasant farmer and fisherman. On that fateful day, he had gone into the forest in search of palm kernels and fruits to be sold for profit in order to provide for his family. Unknown to him, he stepped on a poisonous viper that bit him, leaving a poisonous venom in his body. Emeañaa was fortunate to have been heard by a neighbor as he screamed in pain from the snake bite. It was this neighbor who made arrangements for him to be taken to a traditional "medicine man" about two hours away. Unfortunately, before they could get there, Emeañaa died. News of his death dampened my mood so badly that I spent the rest of the day in sorrow and grief. Yet, as sad as the news of his death may sound, this kind and penniless gentleman with neither power nor education was able to make his voice heard. He was a man with a mission. He died needlessly, without access to the immediate medical care that he believed was so important for his village. I had so hoped that he would live to see the opening of this facility but that was not to be. He made his mark, and he left while the ovation was high.

Emeañaa's death reminded me of other similar avoidable losses of life to the community. One such death was Reverend Father Anthony, a fine gentleman who was serving the Obike community at the time he died. After a long day of tireless labors, Fr. retired to get his rest. In the middle of the night he started to experience what seemed to be a heart attack. He was able to reach out to one of his altar servers who immediately lifted him into his car and drove off to Owerri, where he would get medical attention. The distance from Obike to Owerri is approximately 20 to 25 miles, but the horrible state of the roads sometimes makes it a two-to-three-hour ride. Less than halfway through that journey Fr. died. He died serving the community. Fr. could still be alive and serving today if we had this facility. And there are more heart-breaking stories of endless and careless losses of life.

For the vast majority of the members of this community, in this twenty-first century, the only medical care available is to go into the forest in search of leaves and herbs to combine, as a remedy for complicated, and often undiagnosed, illnesses. Needless to say, these types of dangerous experiments commonly end in disaster. Yet, in the absence of any other viable alternatives, those risky options remain their only choice.

A Groundbreaking Event ...

On August 19, 2018, accompanied by four friends from Most Holy Trinity and members of my family, we marked the groundbreaking event for the Divine Mercy medical facility. It was a day to remember. The event, which started with the celebration of the Holy Mass, attracted over two thousand members of the Obike community. The whole town was agog with excitement. For some it was of great interest to see three white men and one white woman for the first time in their lives, while for others it was simply about the mere thought of being able to have the privilege of a medical facility in a completely forgotten community, or maybe it was both. It was a gathering of who's who in the community, beginning with the traditional ruler, Eze Batholomew Mba, who seized the opportunity to address the community, given the uniqueness of the occasion, and the extraordinary sacrifice and generosity of our guests. He pledged to ensure the safety of our American guests during the duration of their visit and assured them of the hospitality of the community. In what many thought was the highlight of a speech by a ruler who is considered by many as very down-to-earth, the king pointed out that some of the most notable recollections of similar visits by Westerners and Europeans to Africa were the ugly experiences of visitors who arrived with weapons and desecrated the land that received them by enslaving her citizens. In total contrast, our current guests arrived with gifts and the promise of a better future for the community. In a surprising revelation, he announced that the town council had decided to honor our esteemed visitors with chieftaincy titles in recognition of their heroic outreach to a community in desperate need. The news was greeted with so much excitement. In another gesture of gratitude, Professor Chieke Ihejirika and Mr. Christian Eke, two eminent sons of Obike, recognized the extraordinary sacrifice made by our Wallingford friends in visiting the Obike community. The rest of the day was one of fanfare, merriment, music, and dancing as the community gathered to celebrate. Children went wild with joy.

The chieftaincy title event was glamorous. On that occasion, the king once again reminded our guests what an extraordinary joy and honor their visit had brought the community. They were each honored with the title of "Friends of the Obike Community." I think our guests had some appreciation of the cultural significance of the event, judging by the pomp and pageantry. Yet, as one of our guests informed me later, the whole experience began to sink in when an airport staffer stopped in shock as he came upon the chieftaincy paraphernalia in his luggage before departure back to the United

States. That discovery, which significantly changed the staffer's attitude toward Bob, played a major role in helping him realize the value of the honor that had been bestowed upon him.

As part of this groundbreaking event, we included a medical mission for the community. Prior to the trip, we had shipped all the medical supplies from the United States, and Dr. Phil Perrino, an optometrist, made sure we had every provision for an open-air eye clinic. He went above and beyond to order eyeglasses and eye drops from everywhere that he could find them. He quadrupled the orders that I had placed and personally paid for them just to make sure we had enough supplies.

In a matter of three days, our medical team was able to see over one thousand patients. At first, we started with an open-air clinic at the proposed site of the medical facility, but inclement weather forced us to relocate to the local church for the remainder of the days. People even came from neighboring towns to receive care. Although this mission was planned for only three days, seeing the enormous need, our volunteer guests solicited to extend it to a fourth day. In fact, they also suggested canceling a sightseeing trip that I had planned for them just to make sure that no one who came to receive treatment left unattended. Even after the fourth day, there were still plenty of people that could not be seen. On the last day of the medical mission, we worked until dark, until it was difficult to still see people's faces in a town with no power supply. I literally forced our American guests, with the help of the security agents, to get in the car so that we could return to our hotel in Owerri. Saying goodbye was extremely difficult. Yet, from the last day of the medical mission until the day they departed Owerri to return to the United States, Dr. Phil saw another fifty patients, who he invited to Owerri. I only recently discovered that Dr. Phil is still crafting lenses and shipping them to people in Owerri and Obike; those whose cases required extra care, even two years after the trip.

Dr. Phil Perrino seeing patients in Obike

There are so many beautiful stories that deserve to be mentioned. One was about a man who, after trying for several days to have his son seen by the doctors without success, and despite taking out his frustration on me, came back to thank our guests for their selfless generosity. It is a story that goes to show that the majority of the people do not feel entitled, but rather grateful for even the opportunity of care. A related story is that of a man, in his mid to late fifties, who had a foreign body removed from one of his eyes. Apparently, he had this discomfort for his entire adult life, yet without any means of support or available facilities, he was condemned to live with the condition. I have no idea what it was that Dr. Phil did, but he was able to skillfully remove that foreign body out of his eye. This fellow went wild with joy. He ran across the entire village in jubilation proudly showing off his refurbished eyes. It's hard to remember how many times he came to tell me to please thank Dr. Phil and the rest of our guests for him. The whole experience was simply spectacular in every sense of the word. Even our volunteer guests who had no medical experience like Bob, Kim, and Deacon Joe or "Big Joe," as the people nicknamed a man that they immediately fell in love with due to his size or his beard or both, were hands-on issuing cards, writing people's names, getting them to fall in line, taking vital signs, or simply comforting them. As I think about that experience, what comes to mind is what Pope Francis said about a true shepherd, as one who perceives the smell of his sheep. Although these amazing friends of mine are not pastors in the exact sense that the Pope meant that, they acted like shepherds of a sort. They did indeed "smell" the people, embrace them, empathize with them, commiserate with them, and certainly rejoiced with them, for even in the midst of their sorrows there was still plenty of joy and gratitude. While we were in Obike, as the medical mission continued, we also took the opportunity to renovate two homes for two widows, Susanna and Rita, in order to provide them with some comfort. Paula and Clem Ehoff, our board vice president and treasurer, respectively, paid for these renovations.

As we were returning to Owerri from Obike, the skies let loose and it rained uncontrollably. On an already horrible road, it became harder to figure out where the flood started and where the gutters began. We simply were driving blind and at one point we had to pay some locals to show us the right way to direct our tires to avoid ending up in the gutters. In the end, about twenty to twenty-five miles took us over three hours before arriving at our hotels in Owerri. That, plus the fact that each day, on our way to and from Obike, we were forced to exit the vehicle and walk across a bridge and a huge gully erosion site, to avoid falling into a hole, added to the memories from that experience.

We began our visits to the three orphanages that DMIWOO supports the day following the medical mission. In each of the three places we had the most amazing experiences. We met with the nuns who were directly in charge of the orphans as well as the rest of the staff. Perhaps our most memorable experience was playing soccer with the orphans, all of whom played barefoot. Yet, they tackled us fearlessly. Their determination to win was such fun to watch, simply indescribable. They played as if there was a gold medal to win. When we had planned the trip, Mary and Bob Hughes were thoughtful enough to purchase soccer balls, pumps, and goal posts, which were exactly what the kids needed. It was such fun that we had a hard time leaving them. Being able to hold the babies in our hands was phenomenal. It felt indeed like mission accomplished. By the time we were leaving the children had letters they had written for us to bring back to our sponsors and supporters here in the United States. And certainly, they requested that we please come back to visit them again.

The King and Chiefs of Obike honoring our Wallingford guests

Phil, Kim, Bob and Joe in Obike

CHAPTER SIX

The Challenges Back Home ...

Not long after construction started, things began to get out of control. I received reports that people were stealing some of the building materials. I could not believe that anyone would ever imagine trying to sabotage a project that would bring such unparalleled transformation to the community. Upon closer investigation, I found out that it was a bunch of hungry and misguided individuals who thought they could make a few extra bucks by selling our building materials at give-away prices. While I had no way to determine our engineers' involvement or noninvolvement in that sad story, I was disappointed that he could not prevent it from happening. As he realized that I no longer had confidence in him, he offered to resign, and I did not think twice in accepting his resignation. I made sure that all those who were involved in the theft were duly arrested and detained. The community leadership was so outraged that they immediately came out with policies that stipulated severe punishments for any future violators. The community also set up a project monitoring committee led by the traditional ruler, Eze

Batholomew Mba, and other illustrious members of the community, including Christian Eke, Cyprian Amadi, Ben Nworgu, and Charles Okereafor, among others. It really was a disappointing experience, but it was heartwarming to see the leadership of the community step up to the plate in the way that they did.

Architect Chinwe Obihara to the Rescue— Want to Get Something Done, Ask a Woman

The saying that when one door closes God opens another could not have been more true. Chinwe Obihara Ilouno, a brilliant young woman from Umuovumoke Ulakwa was like a round peg in a round hole, in the right place at the right time. At the recommendation of my dear cousins, Julie and Mary, who had been quite resourceful and extremely supportive of our efforts, she stepped in and took over. And from that moment onward I could go to bed in peace in the knowledge that someone truly competent and trustworthy was in charge. Considering the fact that she developed the plan, she understood the intricacies of the building like no other. And there was something profoundly and psychologically remarkable about her taking on the role of a project manager. In a predominantly patriarchal culture, where women play subordinate roles, to see a woman take charge of such a gigantic project was particularly delightful. In stepping into that position, she filled three important roles—namely, a brilliant architect, a project manager, and a role model for women. All this is to say that she was not just hired for an affirmative action in favor of women or just to patronize the woman folk, she was hired because she stood so tall among her peers, men and women alike. Although Chinwe would constantly tell me that her husband is a far better architect, on her own, she leaves nothing to be desired. Chinwe is the kind of architect and project manager that any project owner needs to have. Hers is pure talent, matched with unequalled dedication. She acts with a confidence and calmness that is second to none. My life became a lot easier the day Chinwe took over the project, and I no longer had to worry about whether things were going to be done the right way or not. Most importantly, she immediately understood, unlike most, that what we were doing was *Opus Dei*, which requires the contribution of everyone, including hers. The consciousness that we are doing God's work has been evident in literally everything that she has done to execute this project. Unlike a professional architect, who would be in it just to make money, Chinwe was a professional who would do whatever she could to make this facility available to a community in need. Like the rest of us, Chinwe started to see her role as part of her contribution to saving lives. As the old saying goes, *the reward for every good work is more work.*

During my 2019 trip to Obike, I visited one of the widows that we support. It was heartbreaking to see the squalor in which Chinenye and her five children lived. It was an uncompleted building that had been abandoned for nearly ten years due to lack of money. It had walls that were on the verge of collapse and no roof except for dry raffia palm branches that substituted for a roof. A subhuman condition, to put it mildly. As soon as I returned to the United States, I could not help but share that experience with my dear friend Sharon Healey. Sharon immediately decided that she was going to complete the widow's house, which was more like building it from scratch. All I needed to do was make a phone call to Chinwe and the rest was history. In a matter of a couple of months, working as though it was a mandate from heaven, Chinwe was able to give this woman and her 5 children a brand new home thanks to the generosity of the

Healeys. By the time that project was completed, "Aunt Chinwe," as the village kids called her, had become a household name in the village. Children would recognize her arrival just by the sound of her vehicle, and before anyone knew it, they had congregated from all over the village to say hello to Aunt Chinwe. On the day of the opening and blessing of the widow's house, I watched in complete awe as the children were falling over each other to be the first to get a hug from Aunt Chinwe. And while they did that, they had assorted types of home-grown fruits which they had brought to Chinwe as a sign of their fondness and appreciation. It was such a joy to see someone give and receive so much love in return. As we concluded the Mass that preceded the blessing of the house, which the Healeys built for Chinenye and her children, the whole town rose in prayer, invoking God to bless Architect Chinwe Ilouno for having brought so much joy to the community.

I was extremely pleased to see the level of appreciation and collective celebration in that community on behalf of the one fortunate widow who was gifted with a new home. It was especially remarkable because nearly all the women were just as destitute as Chinenye, who got the new home. She was simply fortunate to have been chosen from among many like herself. Yet, the rest of the community was so full of joy and gratitude for the favored one. It speaks to their beautiful character, the lack of envy, the willingness to rejoice for and with a neighbor, and the hope that kindness attracts kindness. It took the tremendous generosity of the Healey family and the gentle devotion of Chinwe to bring out these beautiful traits from a people who never cease to smile even as they continue to suffer untold hardships.

Project C.U.R.E

Although we had barely commenced construction, I began with the end in view. I started to look into options for the provision of medical equipment to the facility once construction had been completed. I prayed to God for insight and then I randomly went on an online search for possible resources. A variety of organizations popped up, but I chose the first one, Project C.U.R.E. I could not have been more impressed by what I read about their work all around the globe, how they have helped to provide hundreds of medical facilities with equipment amounting to hundreds of millions of dollars. At first, it sounded too good to be true, yet I picked up my phone to call their outlet in Pennsylvania. An extremely kind lady answered my call and took time to educate me on the phenomenal work of this organization and the services they have been providing all over the world for decades. I did not conclude that call without first scheduling a date when I would go on a tour of one of the warehouses from where they shipped their medical equipment. Meeting Kathleen in person was even better than the very inspiring telephone conversation that encouraged me to take the trip. She patiently showed me around the facility, and inside the warehouse where they had various equipment ready to ship. She also talked to me about the process of acquiring these products from various hospitals and manufacturers all across the United States. Finally, she walked me through the application process which sounded quite rigorous yet necessary for the kind of return that would come from the effort. Kathleen informed me that the hoped-for donations would be worth over $400,000. It certainly doesn't get better than that, I thought to myself. At the time when we had this conversation, we had not placed one brick upon another and yet we were required to have completed at least 70% of the project before applying.

So, at that point it seemed like a long shot and a distant possibility. But as they say, knowledge is power. The knowledge that there was such a resource out there was like a big boost to my enthusiasm. I had spent nearly one hour with Kathleen touring the facility and just as I was about to leave, out of nowhere, two women arrived. They were listening to my conversation with Kathleen. They heard me mention the Sacred Heart Church in Oxford, which happened to be their parish, and they remembered that they had heard me speak about the DMIWOO project at their church. These two holy ladies, who volunteered their services at this warehouse, assisting with packing medical equipment for shipment, had donated to the DMIWOO project during one of my visits to their church. What a small world. Kathleen was pleasantly surprised that the women had recognized me, and that helped to put me on a stronger footing with her. We went on almost another hour talking about my outreach to the Sacred Heart church and how their generous support had continued to advance the project. In the end Kathleen became interested in attending any future events at the Sacred Heart so she could hear more about our project, and indeed, a few months later, she attended an outreach event we held in that church.

But something else happened. We also realized as we chatted, unknown to both of us, that my nephew, Nnamdi, who is currently at Pittsburgh Medical School had once volunteered at that very facility, helping to sort products for shipment. Any remaining doubt that I was a real person with real connections and a real need were erased. As I left the facility that day, Kathleen said to me, "I am here for you, Father, whenever you are ready." And yes indeed, by the time we were ready for the shipment, three years later, they would deliver on their promise. It seemed so surreal, like a beautifully choreographed process by He who alone has the power to do such things, the Supreme Intelligence.

However, although Project C.U.R.E donates equipment they do not pay for the shipment. So, we had to look for a way to raise almost $40,000 to ship and deliver a 40-foot container of medical equipment to Obike.

CHAPTER SEVEN

Rotary International (RI)

At the invitation of the amazing Kathy Dawson, one of our board members, I went to speak to the Rotary Club of Westfield, New Jersey, about the DMIWOO clinic project. I was accompanied by former board members George and Kim Marinelli. It was a speech very well received by a group of gentlemen and ladies who were zealous for good works. The club members had such kind compliments for our ministry. Although they did not donate a lot of money on that day, they came up with a beautiful idea, which was to help us apply for the Rotary Foundation grant. Ideas, they say, rule the world. Dr. Michael Hart who suggested this initiative had been a member of the Rotary Foundation for several years. He also promised to investigate all the requirements for application and to guide us through the process, and he did. Also deserving of particular mention here is Liz Ensslin, who was the club president at the time, for her commitment toward the realization of the grant. Liz went out of her way to seek out other rotary clubs to support the grant at a time when it seemed like we had arrived at an insurmountable roadblock. Clark Lagemann who was responsible for applying and processing the grant was, to say the least, outstanding. For the nearly two and half years that the application process lasted, Clark and I were in constant communication, poring over document after document, completing paperwork, following up with people in Nigeria and the United States, sending several emails and making telephone calls, until we were able to receive the funds from the Rotary International and pay for the services toward the shipment of the container of medical equipment. I am eternally grateful to Clark and other willing collaborators for their perseverance and for believing in the DMIWOO project.

The Rotary Club of Westfield, New Jersey, not only contributed money to initiate that grant application as the process required, they also got a number of other Rotary Clubs to contribute so that, cumulatively, we would get more money from the contributions of various clubs combined. With all this interest and assistance, the process went smoothly in the United States. Yet, without the involvement of a host Rotary Club in Nigeria we would not be able to formally apply for the international grant.

With much effort, I was able to identify a host Rotary Club in Nigeria willing to partner with the New Jersey club. Being the host club also implies a number of responsibilities, including visiting the construction site to verify the existence of the project, completing a needs assessment form, and, of course, making a financial contribution to the project. It took nearly a year and a half to complete all these steps, and believe me, those were the longest and most exasperating year and a half of my life. The leadership of the Owerri club at the time we initiated the process was quite supportive. As soon as that administration left, having completed their tenure, either because there was no proper handover or there was lack of interest on the part of the new administration, or both, the process came to a standstill. The Rotary Club of Westfield sent a series of emails requesting information from the Owerri club to no avail. Having waited for over one year without a positive response from Nigeria, the New Jersey club decided to withdraw their support. Their withdrawal led to a domino effect in that the rest of the Rotary clubs in the United States that had pledged to support our application also withdrew. It took an unimaginable number of meetings, emails, and telephone calls to convince the lead Rotary Club in New Jersey that had initiated the grant to reconsider their decision. By the time they did it was already too late to get the clubs that had withdrawn to join back in, as they had now applied their funds to other projects. Many honorable members of the Owerri club were so frustrated that there was such reluctance on the part of the leadership of their club to support a beautiful project and they spoke vehemently against such antipathy. In the end, at the very last minute, the Owerri club managed to complete and submit the application before the extended deadline. We are happy to have been worthy of receiving their support as the Rotary Club is a very reputable organization that continues to do a lot of good all around the world. I do hope that the good people who join this club will continue to manifest in their choices and actions, the motto of this noble organization: "Service above self."

Back in the United States, I confronted the challenge of convincing other Rotary clubs to support the grant application, having lost the ones that had earlier pledged to do so. In one night, I sent more than fifty emails to various Rotary Clubs. The day after that I made countless telephone calls and, subsequently, I had in-person meetings with members of some of these clubs. All this to get clubs to support our application. Eventually, the West Hartford Rotary Club, through an email from their district grant coordinator, Eileen Rau, agreed to contribute to the grant. The way the Rotary International grant works is via the aggregation of funds from various local and district clubs. Given that it is a matching grant, the more clubs you get to support the application by contributing, the larger the amount of money that you are eligible to receive from Rotary International. We were fortunate to have at least two Rotary Clubs in the United States support us. The Rotary Foundation grant made a significant contribution that supported the shipment of our medical equipment to Obike. I am deeply grateful to all the Rotary Clubs and their leadership that helped to make that grant possible. The work that Rotary International does all round the globe remains one of the most remarkable contributions to human development.

Arise, O Compatriots!

Meanwhile, as I was waiting for the Rotary grant to be approved, I decided to explore other options, just in case it didn't happen. In fact, as a result of the apparent lack of enthusiasm from the Owerri club I had started to feel less and less confident about getting it. So, I decided to reach out to the Nigerian community here in the States for support. My immediate plan was to reach out to the community in Pennsylvania and for a good reason. Although I live in Connecticut, the rest of the Ihejirika clan in America, numbering over twenty, live in Pennsylvania. Thanks to their long years of residence in the city of brotherly love and other neighboring cities, they have been able to become part of a vibrant Nigerian American community, both religious and secular, whose respect and admiration they had earned. The Ihejirikas have been presidents of both religious and cultural organizations and have, in the footsteps of our father, done so with honor and distinction. I opted to leverage their good reputation, social capital, and immense network of friends to solicit support for our work. Not surprising, when I shared my plans with them on a conference call, they were extremely supportive of the idea. With their help, I was able to put together a committee of reputable Nigerians to help raise funds for our medical facility. To my list of names, they added a few more who they thought would be a good fit for the committee. Subsequently, I made a trip to Pennsylvania to meet with the group and I could not have been more impressed. I shared the DMIWOO mission and vision with them, as well as the role which I was inviting them to play, and it was all very well received. Over the next couple of months, we would meet via conference calls or over Zoom, for two or more hours every week, to plan a fundraiser. It was the most amazing and incredibly motivated set of people that you could imagine. They started to brainstorm all kinds of ideas until we settled for an in-person fundraising event to be held in Pennsylvania as the best way to proceed. We immediately set the ball rolling. Without any delay, the committee members started making monetary contributions in order to pay for the anticipated costs for the hosting of the event. Besides money, each person voluntarily took on a role to play in the realization of our overall goal. Through a series of meetings, the group identified a remarkable number of generous individuals within the community who they thought would be willing to throw their financial weight behind the project. I sent letters to over fifty individuals that were identified, followed by personal calls. Each committee member was also assigned several guests with a mandate to motivate them enough to attend the fundraising event. Everything seemed all set and ready to go when, sadly, the world got hit hard by the deadly pandemic of COVID-19, which led to the cancellation of our in-person event.

Undiscouraged, the group continued to meet every fortnight in hope that things might improve to a point where we could organize an in-person event, until it became obvious that it wasn't to be. Once we came to that conclusion, this relentless group of patriots, plus one American and a dear friend, decided to switch to a virtual event. At first, we were quite skeptical about it, unsure how our potential guests would respond. As soon as members of the committee became comfortable with the idea, and even enthusiastic about it, we decided to give it a shot. Switching to an online event had both opportunities and challenges. It would require, first, that we would come up with a new date and then reach out to our guests once again to invite and encourage them to attend. We would also need to figure out how to navigate the challenges of organizing such a potentially big and unconventional event, including all the foreseeable and unforeseeable technological glitches. On the flip side, the good news was that we would not have to worry about renting a hall or serving food to our guests, or even cleaning after the event, all of which would help to drive down our costs. It also meant that I would not have to drive from Connecticut to Pennsylvania, a travel time of approximately four hours, to attend the event. Also, being a virtual event, we would not need to restrict it to only people in Pennsylvania, which could mean more participation. That realization turned it into quite an exciting idea. So, we each went to work, well-motivated by the prospect of success. It didn't take long for us to come up with a new date and a new and broader guest list. Like the previously planned in-person event, I called every single person on the guest list, with many kindly responses to my call. A few days prior to the event we began to receive generous financial pledges, which we all interpreted as a very good sign. From among the thirty-six people who attended the Zoom event, and some who simply sent in their contributions, we were able to raise over $25,000. We went into the event both nervous and hopeful, but certainly not thinking that it would be as successful as it turned out. It was by every measure a hugely successful event, especially since it happened at a time when most people had been affected economically and otherwise by the pandemic. It was also a lesson on the need to trust in God, no matter what the circumstances may be. People called in not only from Pennsylvania but also from Texas, Florida, Chicago, Maryland, Virginia, New Jersey, Connecticut, Washington State, and more. Many of these were people who would not have attended the event or contributed if we had held it in person as originally planned. God does indeed have a sense of humor. Reflecting upon that experience now, it makes me really appreciate the saying that, *Not all storms that you encounter come to disrupt your life, some indeed do come to clear your path.* My unquantifiable gratitude goes to all the incredible members of that committee, namely: Dr. and Mrs Obioma Aguocha, Kenechukwu Ilonze, Chief Adol Ibe, Nkiru Uduma, Chisom Orji, Innocent Onwubiko, and my dear friend Annette Reyman, who also happens to be the board Secretary of DMIWOO. I also do not take for granted the sacrifices of my dear brothers Chieke and Emmanuel, as well as my amazing sister-in-law Annunciata. While our oldest brother, Leonard, could not attend our committee meetings, he and his dear wife Florence worked behind the scenes to provide support, and so did my incredible sister-in-law Chioma. Other family and friends who were incredibly supportive during this period include Anthonia, Ify, Too, Kene, Chimmy, and Fr. Chimezie. All are such great champions for the people of Obike. May God bless them all immensely.

CHAPTER EIGHT

It Takes a Competent Board ...

The DMIWOO board is blessed with incredibly talented professionals and good people, with an incomparable passion to make the world, and in particular Obike community, a better place. None of our proud accomplishments would have been possible without them. One of the most remarkable things about our group of board members is that they are not just there to ensure that we made judicious use of our donor's contributions. While it is hard to overstate the sacrifice of their time and their fiduciary responsibilities as board members, they are just as generous with their money as they are with their time.

I shared a little bit about my encounter with Paula and Clem Ehoff which led to the registration and incorporation of DMIWOO in the United States. At the time when I met Paula, she was the Chief Operating Officer at the Westfield Young Men's Christian Association, a.k.a "Y." Paula has many years of experience in nonprofit operations, having previously taught classes in business administration at the University level. Leveraging her vast experience, we were able, as soon as we became incorporated as a 510(c)(3) nonprofit, to hit the ground running without needing to hire an expert in nonprofit operations. Many of the skills that she had acquired over the course of several years from working at the Y became huge assets to benefit a nascent organization. As the board vice president, Paula handles, with a level of efficiency that is second to none, all our correspondence. She also makes sure to keep us in line as far as nonprofit best practices are concerned. Paula holds our vision to provide support to impoverished widows and orphans and remains open-minded in embracing the need for comprehensive support for the entire community, including the provision of health care since, in the end, it will help the widows and orphans thrive. And as I stated earlier, health is wealth. Paula was able to convince her generous friend from Maryland, Dennis Chyba, to build our first website at zero cost, and she also got her daughter, Katti Fields, to manage the website. Katti has been another member of the Ehoff family whose silent contributions to the progress of DMIWOO could hardly be quantified. Besides sponsoring one of our orphans in honor of her son, Cole, Katti continues to provide technical assistance to DMIWOO as often as the need arises. To have Paula as a board member and co-founder is one of the greatest blessings of DMIWOO.

To successfully operate a nonprofit in the United States, you need the level of skills and expertise that Paula's husband, Clem, brings. As a CPA in accounting, Clem is our board treasurer, responsible for making sure that our financial practices are in line with the policies and procedures of the Internal Revenue Service. Clem is also a Professor of Accounting at Washington State University. We are blessed to have him to be able to keep us in check as far as the dos and don'ts of accounting procedures. Clem is also responsible for making sure that funds are made available in a timely manner for the continuation of our projects which, being an international endeavor, can be challenging at times. It was very disappointing to see Paula and Clem move from the northeastern United States to the West Coast, knowing that I would not be able to pay them my occasional visits and to see their cute little puppies. However, we have made sure that our friendship continues to thrive despite the distance.

I met Annette and her husband Michael about the same time when I met Paula and Clem and in the same parish. It has been twelve years now and our friendship has only grown stronger. Before joining the board, where she serves as the executive secretary and chair of the technology committee, Annette was a volunteer who would travel several miles to attend our events. I made many unsuccessful attempts to convince Annette to join the board, yet she continued to provide her services as a volunteer. Once she made the decision to become a board member, she gave it her all. As the chair of the technology committee Annette has introduced some changes that have enhanced the way we do business as an organization. Since joining the board, she has proven that my confidence in her, which made me ask her several times before she finally agreed to serve, had not been misplaced. Perhaps it is one of those burdens that come with being a dependable friend, I feel like I can always approach Annette with any request pertaining to the DMIWOO project, and sometimes with personal needs, and she hardly ever disappoints. Her loyalty and commitment to our mission has been simply phenomenal. And while he is not officially a board member, Annette's husband and my friend, Michael, has also demonstrated, in word and deed, that he is one of the most zealous supporters of the DMIWOO project. I shall continue to pray to God to bless them both immensely for their extraordinary generosity.

Kathy Dawson has served on the board of DMIWOO from

the time we became a registered nonprofit. Kathy is also one of the few that have been with the DMIWOO organization from the very beginning, having been present on the day we launched the organization at the Garwood home of the Ehoffs. To this day, Kathy's excitement, hopes, and enthusiasm for this organization have only grown. In keeping with her position as the director of administration at the Westfield YMCA, Kathy was appointed to take on the role of administrative committee chair where she has served with such diligence. In addition to her incredible skills, Kathy brings such passion to the DMIWOO project that is second to none. One of the greatest optimists that I know, Kathy believes that we can accomplish whatever we set our minds to if we gave it our best shot and if we leave things in God's hands, in total trust and complete abandonment to his will. I cannot tell you how many times that I have fallen back on her inspiring words of encouragement in order to get through rough times, both in matters pertaining to the organization and in things pertaining to myself personally. Her restless desire is that there may be endless opportunities for us to continue to expand our services to a suffering community. Kathy has been such a huge blessing to our board, and I pray God to bless and reward her immensely.

Marcia Meehan is another board member whose wealth of experience at the YMCA has benefited DMIWOO. Marcia has also worked as a capital campaign manager for various nonprofit corporations. Currently our Development Committee Cochair, in the fundraising capacity, Marcia brings a level of expertise in fundraising that many organizations can only dream about. She has been the leading board member in educating the rest of our board on the most effective ways to continue to motivate donors. One of her most recent efforts was when she flew into Connecticut from Virginia to attend our annual board meeting and to make a presentation to the board on the most effective fundraising strategies. Credit to Marcia, we have what we call seven-point touch approaches, which are creative ways to stay in touch with our donors throughout the year. I cannot tell you how incredibly effective that has been. Marcia was a leading donor to our water project in Obike and was also greatly resourceful in trying to get other Rotary Clubs to support our grant application. DMIWOO is exceedingly blessed to have her on our board and we are deeply grateful for her services.

Laurie Reinmann serves on the DMIWOO board as the Development Committee Cochair— Marketing Capacity. Laurie will be remembered, among other things, as the person who initiated the first fundraiser for our medical facility. Together with her amazing husband, Tom, and their two beautiful daughters, Lauren and Katie, they have spearheaded one fundraiser after another, all in an effort to see that the medical facility got built. Laurie is such a go-getter, ever willing to fight her heart out once she believes in something. Her marketing skills have been invaluable assets in helping us reach a significant number of donors who have come through for us in very generous ways. As someone with a considerable level of knowledge of the medical field, thanks to her work with doctors and pharmaceutical industries, Laurie understands more than most the urgency to provide medical services to a people in need and she has demonstrated that commitment in numerous ways. Having Laurie as a board member is more like getting two for the price of one. Her husband Tom has shown an equal amount of commitment to the DMIWOO mission. For our rummage sale, which was one among several fundraising initiatives spearheaded by the Reinmanns, Tom went from home to home picking up donated items and bringing them back to his garage where the event took place. And prior to that was a car wash fundraiser, which was literally held in the rain and under very freezing temperatures, also championed by them, just to mention but a few. We are blessed to have them both and I pray God to bless and reward them immensely.

Bob and Mary Hughes were among the group of friends who gathered the very first day when I invited friends and parishioners of Most Holy Trinity parish in Wallingford to discuss the clinic project. From that day until now they have remained among the most loyal friends and supporters of DMIWOO. Both staff members of the prestigious Yale University in Connecticut, Bob and Mary bring vast experiences and skills sets to bear on the administration of DMIWOO. While Bob works as the Operations Manager at the Cushing Whitney Medical Library, where his main areas of responsibility are finances, facilities, and security, Mary works as the Library Service Assistant and has been at the Yale Medical Library for over fifteen years. Bob serves on the DMIWOO board as the Finance Committee Cochair, while Mary serves as the Program Committee Chair, responsible for providing oversight responsibilities relative to our projects in Nigeria. Thanks to their passion and commitment Mary and Bob have been able to attract family and friends to continue to support the DMIWOO project. From their older son Tommy who volunteered to build a new website for DMIWOO to their younger son Billy, who once provided me with a very thoughtful piece of advice at a very critical decision-making moment, the entire Hughes family has been all in as far as their support for DMIWOO. They, the Reinmanns, and the Healeys, are among the few who have been a part of many of the fundraisers for our medical facility.

Bob was among the first who approached me and expressed an interest in travelling with me to Nigeria for the groundbreaking event, and since that trip, which he describes as life changing, he has been relentless in making sure that we delivered on a promise that we collectively made to the Obike community. In addition to everything else, Bob and Mary's relationship with a motherless young man called Remigius (Chigemezu) who Bob fell in love with during his Nigerian trip, and who they both consider their adopted third child, has continued to provide them with an undying affinity with the Obike community. These years of my association with the Hughes family have taught me that empathy for the oppressed and the marginalized is something that is intrinsic to who they are, which was why identifying with the DMIWOO mission seemed like a matter of course for them.

Besides serving as board members, which is very important to me, Bob and Mary's friendship has been an incredible source of support for me personally, in both good and challenging times. Their home is one place where I could easily go to hang out or enjoy a good meal over a glass of Moscato. Their sense of loyalty to any person or cause with which they identify is inimitable, which makes them some of the most honorable people that I know. You could see a test of their loyalty in the fact that despite having lived in Connecticut for over thirty years, they remain, in Bob's words, "avid Buffalo Bills and Sabres fans." They both are such a blessing to the DMIWOO ministry, and I pray God to reward them immensely.

Professor Chieke Ihejirika started out as the founding board secretary before he transitioned to the role of board Nigerian ambassador. As our Nigerian ambassador, he acts as a liaison officer for the board, keeping us abreast of the political and economic situation in Nigeria in a way that we can navigate effectively the similarities and differences, challenges and opportunities, that are likely to emerge while operating in two vastly different sociocultural and political environments. His vast experiences in both cultures, plus his outstanding background in academia, having taught history, political science and philosophy at Lincoln and other universities for several years, makes him a huge asset for the board. As someone who had been there from day one, he is as familiar with the history and development of the DMIWOO organization as anybody else including myself. As a matter of fact, his efforts were precursors to our current accomplishments, having previously worked with his colleagues and friends at the Lincoln University to provide potable water to a community in need. His water project was subsequently expanded by DMIWOO so that water is available to the most vulnerable members of the community. It is a privilege to be blessed with a brother of his pedigree and someone whose knowledge, experience, and passion for positive change, on behalf of the Obike community, makes him an added voice of hope for a people in need. I could not have asked for a more supportive brother and friend.

Professor Emmanuel Ihejirika is also a founding board member and financial secretary of DMIWOO. As a professor of accounting and finance, as well as the coordinator of graduate business programs at the Lincoln University, he is part of a group of three that make up our finance committee, a subgroup within the board. Besides serving on the larger board, which meets once a month via teleconference and once a year in person, every board member is appointed to serve on a separate committee which meets as the need arises, in order to deliberate on issues to be taken on by the board at our monthly plenary sessions. This model, our board believes, makes for greater efficiency while avoiding the unnecessary prolongation of board meetings. Emmanuel is also cochair of the technology committee. He brings with him advanced accounting skills in ways that hugely benefit our board. As someone who is also a product of both cultures, he enjoys a vintage position on the board to provide some cultural awareness in areas where it may be required. His conversance with the situation in Nigeria added to our mutual passion to improve the well-being of the people at home makes him a great asset to the DMIWOO organization. He is another brother and friend in whom I am well pleased.

DMIWOO Board and Volunteers

CHAPTER NINE

A Roll of Honor

Sharon, Paul, and Daniel Healey

L et me preface this part by saying that I am deeply grateful to any and everyone who has made any contributions in cash or kind toward the advancement of the DMIWOO. Like an anthill, each of your sacrifices in time, talent, and treasure has added up to the huge success that we have accomplished. You all belong in this roll of honor.

But I want to take a moment to mention a few individuals who went above and beyond to bring us to where we are today. The Healeys were the first to reassure me that this project, which at first seemed like a long shot, could indeed be realized. As I flew back from my trip to Nigeria in January 2016, having acquired a large piece of land for the construction of our medical facility, it was a mixture of both joy and uncertainty. While I felt greatly motivated by the community fundraisers that we had organized and which gave me the initial hope and motivation, I often wondered whether it was indeed possible to raise the huge amounts of money required for the construction of the medical facility. Yet, in my wonder and uncertainty, I prayed. I returned to a huge pile of mail in my room that cold January evening, having been gone for a relatively long time. I typically do not rush to open my mail upon return from a long trip, but this time was different. While I still had my suitcases to unpack and trying to catch my breath, I decided to open my mail. The first letter I grabbed and opened was from Sharon and Paul Healey— what a pleasant surprise! Enclosed was a huge check. So huge that my heart skipped a beat. That was totally unexpected. Hoping that I might still find more surprises, I decided to open every single letter, and there were lots of them. I was not disappointed. There was another generous check from a different donor and several small Christmas gifts to me by my incredibly kind parishioners. I kind of thought I knew who the Healeys were, but I wasn't exactly sure. It would take days before I was able to properly identify who they were and that made me even more surprised. I had prayed to God intensely on my nearly 24-hour journey back to the United States, asking him to not allow this community in Obike, that responded with such enthusiasm and with such incredible generosity, to be let down. That donation from the Healeys indeed seemed like an answered prayer. From that moment, they have been relentless in their peerless generosity with their time, talents, and treasure. They would match our rummage sale, doubling the amount, out-buy everyone at our auctions, donate to online fundraisers in huge amounts, pay for halls for our events, donate gift baskets in large numbers to be auctioned, collect and organize the shipment of various items to assist people in Nigeria. The list goes on and on. One year, following their shocking donation, in honor of my birthday, the Healeys surprised me with another generous donation. Not only that, Sharon reached out to another mutual friend of ours, encouraging him to match their donation, and he did, leading to a most generous birthday surprise to me in favor of DMIWOO. Many generous donors would simply give you money and walk away, not so with the Healeys. Sharon Healey has been so hands on that you could hardly guess that she and her family would be capable of making such big dollar donations. She would be the first one to volunteer to decorate halls for DMIWOO events, clean up after an event, or simply pledge her services wherever they may be needed, an attitude which speaks to their incredible humility on top of everything else. When we started our weekly bingo to raise money for the construction of the medical facility, Sharon was among the first to volunteer every single week for the running of that event. She would come hours earlier than the rest of the group, together with George and Kim, to ensure that everything was in place. And when we made the decision to discontinue bingo, due to low turn-out, she was extremely disappointed and upset that she would no longer be able to help support DMIWOO in that way. Two years ago, I returned from Nigeria and shared a video of a young widow who lived in a squalor with her five children. Sharon immediately approached me expressing an interest in building a house for this unfortunate family and, less than a year later, the Healeys fulfilled that promise. And that was in addition to providing educational scholarships to all five of these children, not to mention a generous business grant to enable this poor widow to stand on her own. The Healeys have been by far the most outstanding supporters of the DMIWOO mission, bringing their friends and family to literally every event. One experience that has remained indelible on my mind was when Sharon's sister Denise, who attended one of our fundraisers, took a fall as she was leaving at the end of the event. As I joined Sharon in helping her injured sister to her car, I was so disappointed and yet so moved by the amount of sacrifice that Sharon, her family, and many others were making for the well-being of a community they have only heard about, and I wonder if love could be more loving. As if they have not already done enough, inspired by my buddy Daniel, the Healeys, the Perrinos, and the Beales are collaborating to build a school in Obike in order to provide greater educational opportunities to more orphans. The Healeys are leaving such a legacy of their huge generosity that will be there for generations to honor. They are indeed an answer to years of prayers. May God bless and reward them immensely.

Daniel Healey

My connection with the Healeys started with their son Daniel. One day, as I was descending from the staircase of the rectory, heading into the kitchen to make myself some breakfast, I saw Daniel. His countenance was so radiant, with such beauty and innocence, that he was simply impossible to resist. Daniel was volunteering his services at the parish, helping to shred documents that had confidential information. My first attempt to say hello to Daniel was not very successful. I was not entirely surprised since it was our first meeting and my first effort to reach out to him. I was a total stranger. His very kind caregiver, who accompanied him on that day, tried but could not succeed in encouraging him to say hello back to me. Over time, however, and probably given my perseverance in trying to reach out and have a conversation with him, Daniel started to reciprocate my overtures until we were able to gradually familiarize ourselves with each other. Although I would naturally acknowledge people, especially if they were providing services to my parish, there was something about Daniel right from the very first minute that I saw him. He had this sublime presence and simply pure beauty about him. He was special in every sense of the word. It's been years now since Daniel and I have been buddies, yet each time I encounter him, I continue to marvel at the grace that radiates through this fine human being. Daniel is a special needs child and the all-knowing provident God entrusted him to the care of the most distinctively loving parents, supremely capable of providing that kind of love deserving of this beautiful child of God.

When I am privileged to spend some time with them, I hear and observe Sharon and Paul cast a loving glance at Daniel, speak of their joys, gratitude and privilege in being his parents, speak gleefully about his daily activities, his jobs and learning experiences, and positively affirm him. They tell indeed how their whole lives are planned around Daniel and I cannot help but think about how their inimitable love for their son is a perfect representation of that beautiful portrait of love, as Saint Paul diligently laid out in his letter to the Corinthians, where: "Love is patient; love is kind. There is no limit to its forbearance, to its trust, its hope, its power to endure. Love never fails" (1Corinthians 13:4–8, *New American Bible*). And yet, despite their constant and loving commitment to their son, or maybe because of it, like a well that is constantly replenished by an infinite source, they remain the most disposed to empty themselves out for others in generosity toward those who suffer.

All parents of special needs children must possess such grace and privilege that the rest of us do not have. It is as though God entrusts them with both responsibility and the charisma that is proportionate to their huge but sacred vocations. I admire their courage and the profundity of their love in living up to this special calling. What we must recognize is that when God sends those special packages, he sends them to those he has specially endowed with the uncommon capacity to treasure, to love, and to honor His most wonderful creation, made in His image and likeness. He sends, indeed, a gift of Himself wrapped in vulnerability. To look after them with so special care is to have taken care of God Himself who reminds us that, "as often as you did it for one of my least brothers, you did it for me" (Matthew 25:40, *New American Bible*). If you are a caregiver to a child with special needs, be they physical or mental, you are in a space that most of us could not be, doing a holy duty for God and for humanity. We all owe you our support and prayers; that the God of all love may reward you with love's greatest rewards.

Fr. Kingsley and buddy, Daniel Healey

Phil and Francie Perrino

Phil and I had a chance encounter one day at the Most Holy Trinity
Parish Center. He had requested me to hear his confession, which
I gladly did. Following that encounter, Phil and I chatted a little
bit about many different things, especially spiritual matters. It was
our first encounter, and I couldn't be more amazed at the depth
of his knowledge of Catholic faith and spiritual matters. I felt like
I was in the presence of a very highly educated Catholic priest or
a college professor of theology. I was also extremely impressed to
hear about his love of music and how, for many years, he has been
a leading voice at Holy Trinity parish's weekly holy hour. Later
on, I would learn about his deep connection with the Legionaries
of Christ with whom he has had many years of association and an
amazing friendship. As Phil left me that evening, he said, "Feel free
to reach out to me, Father, if you need anything." Quite honestly, I
did not think much of that statement which sounded to me more like
something I would often hear from parishioners. But the man was
not kidding, he was not just any parishioner. He was very serious.
The day following my announcement of the DMIWOO clinic
project, Phil and Francie were the very first to go online and make
a generous donation via our website. It was the beginning of an
incredible track record of unparalleled generosity. As soon as Phil was
able to ascertain that our website could receive PayPal donations, he
was unrivalled in making those huge donations using that medium.
Every couple of months, we would find a generous donation with
the Perrino's name on it. Over a short period of time, this extremely
unassuming optometrist had donated tens of thousands of dollars
using our online medium. Phil and Francie, his beautiful wife, who
also happens to be an optometrist, would also give generously to our

fundraising events or even give to promote the event ahead of time. Few families that I know are as effortlessly gracious as the Perrinos. A couple of years ago, Phil and Francie graciously invited me to join their family for Thanksgiving. On that visit, I shared with Phil my worries concerning the shipment of a 40-foot container of medical equipment to Nigeria. A few months later, on the day I was being sworn in as a United States citizen, Phil and Francie presented me with an incredibly generous check in support of that effort. And one of the most amazing things about this couple is that they are never too particular about designating their donations provided you applied them where the need was most urgent. They were the mystery donors that matched the Healey's huge donation, which added to a great birthday surprise. It's hard to keep track of the incredibly generous giving history of the Perrinos to the DMIWOO mission. Yet, our dream of a medical facility would not be what it is today without their support. We owe the huge amount of support that we have received from the extended Perrino family to the great inspiration provided by this amazing couple, Phil and Francie. Phil was also among the seven people who joined me on a trip to Nigeria for the groundbreaking event. Children immediately gravitated toward this fine-looking dude from Connecticut, and he paid a huge price for it. This extremely energetic and deeply enchanted group of children tasked him to run around the arena several times with them to the point that it took my intervention to rescue him from them. Believe me, it was such a lovely sight to behold. After diligently, and with such inspiring patience, taking care of so many who were afflicted with eye diseases, from the simplest to the extremely complicated, Dr. Phil became such a household name in Obike that it has continued to resound more than two years after that medical mission experience to Nigeria. Phil himself would describe that experience as phenomenal. His goal was to make sure that no one was left untreated. Thanks to Phil's insistence, supported by the rest of the group, we had to extend our originally planned two-day medical mission to a third day. And yet, after the third day, I could only manage to get him to join the vehicle waiting to bring us back to our hotel in the city, because in that pitch darkness of a town without electricity, he could no longer see the faces of the people that he so earnestly desired to treat. And while I thought we had concluded what was by every measure an extremely intense week, Phil gave people appointments to come see him at our hotel in Owerri where he would continue his clinical encounters. Going to the orphanages and playing soccer with the kids brought out another side of Phil that I had never seen while in the United States: childlike, lost in the moment, totally joyful. That experience left both the visitors and the kids with lots to remember. It has been two years since our medical mission trip and Phil has continued to maintain a relationship with the young local doctors that he worked with during that mission. I am not sure if Phil returned to the United States with a third of the equipment that he had brought with him to Nigeria, as I saw him on several occasions gifting those young doctors with very sophisticated equipment rarely available in Nigeria. Since returning two years ago, I have also assisted him in shipping those kinds of equipment to support these young doctors who have been deeply inspired by his kindness. In an effort that was spearheaded by my dear friend Karen Brown, Phil was able to join me in a televised interview with the legendary Kevin Nathan, where he reflected on his experiences in Nigeria. That interview also featured another amazing friend, Karen Ripa, whose most recent birthday fundraiser was designated to support the DMIWOO project. Of all things that can be said of any human being, one of the best, in my opinion, is to describe them as good. Phil is a good man in the truest sense of the word. DMIWOO is profoundly grateful to this fine couple, Phil and Francie, for their extreme generosity, and I pray God to pay them back in kind.

Chris and Abby Beale

Chris and Abby have been more like the silent actors behind the scene and yet two of my most trusted and dependable supporters. Chris and I first became acquainted while attending my weekly bible classes at Most Holy Trinity which, he told me, he looked forward to each week. Chris shocked me when he approached me with a very generous check soon after I announced our intention to build a medical facility in Obike. Since that time, Chris and Abby have only gotten more and more generous. Not long after Chris and Abby made that generous donation, I was reassigned to Saint Justin-Saint Michael parish in Hartford, which, as Chris later told me, did upset him so much. However, Chris and Abby made a trip to my new place of residence in Hartford to ask me how they could continue to support the DMIWOO clinic project, and on that trip they made another generous donation. Earlier this year, when it seemed like we were going to run out of funds to continue construction, they added another incredibly large donation so work would not stop. Chris and Abby have also made several generous donations both online and at our events, in their desire to help us fulfill this promise to a community in need. Most recently, they contributed in their typical generous way to ensure that water is made available at the medical facility. Their monetary donations in support of our efforts have been simply unbelievable.

But this couple has also provided another amazing channel of support to me, one that is fundamental to my very well-being. On the very day that they came to visit me in Hartford, while Chris came to see my new place of residence and to pledge their continued support, Abby, who had become aware of my health challenges through Chris, and who is a registered homeopath practicing in Massachusetts, came to converse with me about my health challenges in order to determine how she could help to improve my health and well-being. From that day, Abby has shown such dedication to my continued well-being in a way that is nothing short of humbling. She has provided homeopathic remedies with clear instructions on how to use them, follow up calls, occasional debriefing to de-stress and more. And to think that Abby does all these free of charge is simply amazing. Abby and I have also discussed how these remedies, that have had such a remarkable impact on my overall well-being, could benefit people in Nigeria. Abby would often say to me that she thinks I am doing so much for so many that she feels the need to do whatever she can to support me so I can continue to carry on my ministry to those in need. It is so encouraging to see someone speak and act in such an extremely thoughtful way towards me, and it fills me with such gratitude to know that I have such immensely caring friends. Chris and Abby have been such a blessing to the DMIWOO project and to my life, and I cannot thank them enough. I pray the God of love to grant them love's greatest rewards.

Brian and Diedre Sheehan

My relationship with Brian and Diedre started during my three month assignment in Watertown, Connecticut, at the Church of Saint John the Evangelist. Since I left that parish in 2014 this incredible couple have remained loyal friends to the core and committed supporters of DMIWOO. They have visited me in almost every parish that I have been in since leaving their parish. From the time they learnt about our intention to build a medical facility, Diedre and Brian have attended nearly every event that we have hosted and have made extremely generous contributions. Their passion to support those in need is simply exemplary, and thanks to them and other generous donors, our doors will soon be opened to the public for much-needed medical services. Only very few have given to this project the way that the Sheehans have. My prayers are for God to reward and replenish them a million-fold.

Between these four families, we raised over 50% of the target amount required for our medical facility. The generosity of these families and all the many smaller dollar sacrificial donations only point to the abundance of goodness that has continued to make the United States that "shining city" on the hill, a beacon of hope. It is the character and the spirit of these good and gracious folks that define the American nation.

I also want to take a moment to highlight the contributions of two more heroes, one of whom was on the trip to Nigeria with us. When I proposed the idea of going to Nigeria for the groundbreaking event, many people indicated interest. As they started to do their research and to read more and more about Nigeria, many reconsidered the decision to travel with me. Many of them probably relied on all sorts of information and misinformation, which they found on social media, regarding the danger in travelling to Nigeria. Some even went to the State Department website where they found a note of caution for those thinking about a trip to Nigeria. To be clear, there is no denying that some of the things that they read about Nigeria were factual. And many were simply blown out of proportion. But there was no way to convince them otherwise. The truth of the matter is that Western media is hardly interested in Africa in the same way that they are interested in London and Paris, unless there is some negative news to report. And sadly, negative news is what catches the attention of the masses. Nigeria is a country of over 190 million beautiful people and many cultures, with a significant number of corrupt politicians that have continued to hold the country hostage, enriching themselves, their families, and their cronies at the expense of the poor masses. There is admittedly economic and political crisis in Nigeria.

Yet, against all odds, four friends, Caucasian Americans, had the courage to travel with me, having concluded that the lives of the people there were worth the risk. Besides, if other human beings lived there, I am sure they thought it meant that they too could safely visit that forgotten region of the world. That decision, to me, was simply monumental. It turned out that during our time in Nigeria, the team saw with their own eyes that it is five times more likely for someone to die by violence in many cities across the United States than they are in that region of the world. However, in order to put their minds to rest, I planned for extra armed security officers to be with them for the entire duration of the trip. I have had the chance to write about Kim, Bob and Phil, who were part of the group of four. I would like to talk about one more who made the trip and one who could not.

Deacon Joe Mazurek was the fourth person on that trip. Either due to his notable size or his luxuriant beard which, even in the United States brought him the reputation of "Father Christmas," the entire town fell in love with him at first sight. Joe got a kick out of the fact that on the one day when he decided to take a break and to stay back at the hotel, we left him with an armed security guard who barely allowed him breathing space. That experience may have contributed to why the group requested that I consider getting rid of the law enforcement officers, which they thought was overkill. Besides, they also had seen first-hand the incongruence between Western media portrayal of the security situation in Nigeria and the actual situation. They saw that most of the people lived in relative peace and freedom. The long story in short is that Joe was such a blessing to our team and the impact that his visit made was one with enduring ramifications. Prior to our trip, he and his beautiful wife Karen, who is also one of our volunteers, made a generous donation to support the construction of the medical facility. And while we were in Nigeria, Joe also made another donation to enable us to make more supplies available to the orphanages. It was beautiful to see Deacon Joe proclaim the gospel in Obike on the day of the groundbreaking ceremony.

But there is also another unsung hero, a woman whose courage, tenacity, and yes, her incredible generosity, has continued to inspire me. Bronwen Wrinn is a 77-year-old immigrant from Ireland to the United States. Bron was the second person to approach me with a request to be a part of the mission trip to Nigeria, and she wasn't kidding. She did everything to make that dream a reality. She completed all the paperwork, did all the inoculation and even went with us to New York to get her visa. As soon as her visa was approved, Bron purchased her air ticket, paid for her hotel, had her suitcases ready to go, with lots of goodies for a people she had only heard about. We had all gathered at the location from where we would take off to the airport when we suddenly realized that Bron could no longer walk without support. I was simply dumbfounded. While we were trying to figure out what was going on with Bron, we also found out sadly that the limousine, which we had reserved to bring us to JFK airport in New York, would not be able to accommodate all our suitcases. George Marinelli, God bless him, had to make an unplanned trip to New York JFK to bring the remainder of our suitcases.

It took a lot of people and time to convince Bron that it was not safe for her to join us on a trip in which she had invested so much.

And this was not before she had broken down in tears and literally on her knees begging me not to stop her from making that trip. To watch her cry in that way broke my heart. That decision would rank among one of the most difficult decisions of my entire life, and I hope I never have to face such a situation again. In the end, Bron accepted that the decision was probably in her best interest. So, we made the trip, sadly, without her. Yet, while we were in Nigeria, I took time to publicly acknowledge this extremely amazing woman and the group was kind enough to bring back souvenirs for her.

Bron has remained one of the most formidable supporters of the DMIWOO mission. She volunteers wherever she can and donates as often as her means allows her, in an effort to ensure that we accomplish our goal. Bron's capacity to love, to care, and to give is simply infinite. Although Bron did not get to make that trip, she remains one of my heroes. May God bless her kind and beautiful heart. One may argue that it was probably reckless on the part of the group to have gone on that trip to Nigeria, all things considered. I am not sure how to respond to that. However, is it not true though that love involves some element of recklessness? Doing good at all costs, paying a price for the sake of something or someone you love, or simply making a sacrifice in the name of love, are not those the things that do indeed make love worthy of the name? On this amazing journey, I can tell you, I have seen plenty of those.

I would also like to pay special tribute to a very dear friend and generous supporter of the DMIWOO mission, Francisca Perletti. About a month ago, I woke up early one morning and the first thing that came to mind was to pick up my phone and call this amazing lady. I had not heard from Francisca through the troubling months of the pandemic, so I started to get worried. The message from her answering machine when I called, that her number was no longer in use, got me even more worried. I quickly sent her an email just to make sure that everything was okay, but it wasn't. Less than half an hour later, Francisca's nephew wrote back to inform me that she had passed a couple of weeks ago. It was such sad news to hear. I went in to say Mass that afternoon with a heavy heart and I prayed to God for the repose of her gentle soul. About a month later, I received a brown envelope in the mail from Francisca's attorney in Italy. Francisca had willed a substantial amount of money to me for the continuation of the DIMIWOO mission. Francisca's contribution will be applied in a way that will honor her beautiful memory. I have no doubt that there is now a Saint Francisca Perletti in heaven, praying for the prosperity of DMIWOO.

EPILOGUE

While I have not engaged in this amazing ministry for the reward of it, I cannot deny that *goodness has been its own reward*. I had a near death experience seven years ago. It was an experience that led to six surgeries in a little over three months, in four hospitals. At the time, things seemed so completely hopeless that I concluded, after several surgeries, that my end had come. When my family came to see me in the hospital, prior to being wheeled into the theater for one of my operations, I had concluded that it was more than likely that I was not going to see them again. I also made the necessary spiritual preparations in view of what I thought was inevitable. I requested a very dear friend, Marge Chambers, to arrange for a meeting between me and an attorney who would help to formalize my will, not that I had much that was worth a fight over. At the peak of that dreadful experience, I was airlifted from one hospital to another into the waiting arms of an army of medical professionals, having been previously rejected by no less than three hospitals. Prior to the airlifting, I had survived eight hours of nonstop vomiting of blood, which was only possible due to constant blood transfusion. I do not think that anybody believed that I was going to make it, least of all me. After twelve days at Temple University Hospital, for my fifth surgery in a short period of time, doctors were able to control the excessive vomiting of blood, while stabilizing me to be flown to Bay State medical center in Springfield, Massachusetts, for my sixth operation. As arrangements were being made for that second airlifting to a more specialized hospital, my kidney function failed, which meant that I had to be readmitted for two extra days until my kidneys could function again. It was in this Pennsylvania hospital, as I waited to recover from my fifth surgery, that I got the news that my father had died. As the old saying goes, *when it rains it pours*. Through these health ordeals, including the passing of my father, I had the most immeasurable support of my parishioners, especially Vernette Townsend who was a senior staff of the hospital at the time, and my friend Fr. Emmanuel, at Saint Justin-Saint Michael. Their compassion and love, both material and spiritual, gave me reason to hope and to live.

Considering how feeble I was at the time from multiple surgeries, having lost a lot of weight and still unable to eat normal meals, my doctors advised that it would be unsafe for me to travel to Nigeria for my father's funeral, but that was not a thought I was willing to entertain. After a series of conversations, during which I managed to convince my doctors that going to my father's funeral would have such a therapeutic effect on me, they allowed me to travel. To do so, however, they made sure that I had made extra arrangements for emergency medical insurance while in Nigeria. I barely made it through the funeral Mass, which was attended by over sixty priests and presided over by the Archbishop of Owerri. I also managed to go to the graveside to pay my last respect to my dear father. Beyond that, I am not able to recall what happened for the rest of that long day, full of activities, except that I was escorted to my room at a point when I could no longer stand without support, due to physical and emotional exhaustion. As soon as I began to feel a little better, which was early the following morning, I decided to take a leave from the village to a friend's house where I could rest and rejuvenate. When I returned to the village less than twenty-four hours later, a most memorable thing happened. As I was taking an early morning walk, I saw a large group of widows headed in my direction. While I was still wondering what or who they were looking for, or if they got tipped off that I had returned to the village, these women came running toward me and, in what was the most humbling yet most memorable sight, they all knelt on the ground, with eyes and hands lifted to the heavens, thanking God for saving my life. Tears began to run down my cheeks and theirs like a broken tap. It was quite a scene to behold. These women had heard about my health ordeals and had been praying relentlessly to God on my behalf. Seeing me alive was nothing short of answered prayers. It was particularly interesting that this happened at a time when I had started to say to myself that it was time to step back from some of my self-imposed responsibilities for more self-care. But how could I continue to do that having just witnessed such an immeasurable expression of gratitude. Indeed, contrary to my earlier decision to slow down, that experience became a moment of validation for me, and a reminder that I could not possibly abdicate the responsibility to continue to fight, as best as I can, on behalf of those beautiful women. In that moment, I became even more resolute in my conviction to continue to fight for them and for the orphans. I felt ever more ready.

It has been quite a journey. One with several twists and turns, bends and curves, yet the journey continues. Through it all, I have been bruised and wounded, tried and tested, fell and rose and am still going. Yet, I regret nothing. Through it, I have found meaning and mission, reason and purpose, pain and gain, grace and strength, challenge and opportunity. Yet, I regret nothing. If I had to do it all over, I would not hesitate one bit. Never in a million years would I have imagined that we would be where we are now. I could not imagine that we would be opening, on the tenth anniversary of DMIWOO, a nearly one-million-dollar facility in one of the remotest parts of the world. Yet, it speaks to the power of dreams. Dare to dream, but more importantly dare to pursue your dreams. The future certainly belongs not only to those who can dream but who can relentlessly pursue their dreams. Living a life that matters is living a life with a vision and mission. In the end, it all comes back to the same thing, the one enduring motivation for all my endeavors and my philosophy of life, that, *Unless you live for something you die for nothing.* And the journey continues as I wonder what next ...

To everyone who has inspired or challenged me to get to where I am today, family, friends or even adversaries, my gratitude is immeasurable. I am equally grateful to my terrific parish family of Saint Justin-Saint Michael for their deeply treasured love and support. To all the incredibly generous supporters of DMIWOO, words are grossly inadequate to express how humbled I am for your dedication to this labor of love. When people's lives are touched, they say, God's heart is moved. You have indeed touched several lives. My prayers and blessings will always be with you. My deepest appreciation goes to all my friends and family who took time to read through my manuscript and provided very meaningful feedback, including Annette Reyman, Brenda Delgado, Professor Chimezie Osigweh, Bob Hughes, Professor Chieke Ihejirika, and to my dear friend Kay Taylor-Brooks who assisted with the initial draft for the cover design.

I am deeply grateful to Archbishop Anthony Obinna, who ordained me a priest 18 years ago, and to Archbishop Leonard Blair for granting me the privilege of serving the good people of the Archdiocese of Hartford.

I honor the abiding memory of the irreplaceable Monsignor Theophilus Ibeghulam Okere, who longed for the day when we would open our medical facility to the public. I also honor the ever-loving memory of the Very Reverend Dr. Julius Uroegbulam Mmegwa, who loved and cared for me like a brother. Their memories will forever be a blessing!

To the Almighty, who has done great things for us, who uplifts the lowly and with whom nothing is impossible, be all the glory forevermore.

Divine Mercy Medical Center

Please consider making a donation to support our efforts by going to WWW.DMIWOOO.ORG Or mail your donation to: DMIWOO P.O.Box 156 Ellensburg WA 98926

Printed in the United States
by Baker & Taylor Publisher Services